MW01613278

# The Silver Touch
# and Other
# Family Christmas Stories

Margret Rettich

# The
# Silver Touch
## and Other
## Family Christmas
## Stories

illustrated by Rolf Rettich

translation from the German
by Elizabeth D. Crawford

William Morrow and Company
New York 1978

For everyone in these stories

LIBRARY OF CONGRESS CATALOGING IN PUBLICATION DATA
Rettich, Margret.
The silver touch and other
family Christmas stories.
Translation of Wirklich wahre
Weihnachtsgeschichten.
Summary: A collection of twenty-three
stories relating humorous incidents
that really can happen during
the Christmas holidays.
1. Christmas stories.  [1. Christmas
stories.  2. Short stories]
I. Rettich, Rolf.    II. Title.
PZ7.R3255Si     [Fic]     78-6817
ISBN 0-688-22164-5    ISBN 0-688-32164-X lib. bdg.
Printed in the United States of America.
First Edition
1   2   3   4   5   6   7   8   9   10

# TABLE OF CONTENTS

# The Silver Touch

When Mrs. Mashler was hanging out her wash on the roof, her old neighbor came over to her. She had been rummaging in her storage room.

"I have something for Julie for Christmas," she said.

"How nice of you!" said Mrs. Mashler. "That will certainly please Julie."

The old lady dragged over an object that rattled and squeaked dreadfully. It was an old-fashioned doll carriage. It was bent out of shape and had only three wheels. The fourth lay in the body, where the dolls belonged, along with the hood.

Mrs. Mashler was dismayed when she saw the old wreck, but she didn't feel she could refuse the present. So she thanked her neighbor and took the carriage into her apartment.

After Julie was in bed that night, Mrs. Mashler

7

pushed it into the living room. "Look at this old thing," she said to her husband, who was sitting in front of the television set. "The old lady next door brought it for Julie. The other children will laugh at her when they see it. But what shall I do? The old lady meant well."

Mr. Mashler was not only watching television but reading the paper as well. He mumbled, "Hm, so, yes, yes, hm."

"So you think it's as bad as I do?" Mrs. Mashler continued. "Do you think it would be worth it to fix it up? If I only knew how Julie'd feel about it."

Mr. Mashler was not only watching television and reading the paper, now he also lit a cigarette. He murmured, "Yes, yes, so, so, ffft," and blew out the match.

Mrs. Mashler turned the doll carriage this way and that. The handle was bent and covered with rust. The wickerwork was coming unraveled. The curtains on the hood were mere rags.

"Poor Julie," she said with a sigh, "she's supposed to walk her lovely dolls in a monstrosity like this! But surely the old lady will ask me what Julie said, and then what shall I say?"

Mr. Mashler was not only watching television and reading the newspaper and smoking, now he poured himself a glass of beer. "Hm, hm, hm," he said.

Mrs. Mashler began to pull on the handle until it was fairly straight. She succeeded in fastening on the wheel. She also attached the hood where it belonged and mended the wicker with string. In the kitchen she scrubbed the whole doll carriage with a brush and hot, soapy water. Rummaging in her closet turned up an old petticoat that she hadn't worn for a long time. She used it to line the hood. The lace on the hem made a little frill around it.

Television was over, and Mr. Mashler found no more news in the newspaper. He finished his beer, ground out his cigarette, and came into the kitchen.

"Time for bed," he said. Then he saw the doll carriage. "Wow, what a wild-looking vehicle! Where did that come from?"

"I've told you several times," said Mrs. Mashler, "but you weren't listening."

Mr. Mashler considered the carriage quite presentable, though somewhat colorless. He thought for a minute and then began to search through his tool cupboard, in the bookcase, and at last in the pantry. He found what he was looking for in the broom closet. It was a big can of silver-bronze paint he had bought for his car. He pushed Mrs. Mashler aside and began to silver the frame.

"The wheels too," demanded Mrs. Mashler. She held the paint, and he painted the wheels and then the handle. They both stood there and looked at the carriage with their heads on one side.

"Julie might just like it," said Mrs. Mashler. Mr. Mashler dropped some silver bronze on the hood.

"Look out," cried Mrs. Mashler and tried to wipe it off with her apron. The spot remained. So Mr. Mashler painted the hood silver too.

When that was done, silver bronze had dripped onto the wicker in a number of places. It didn't take long to paint the wicker, and Mr. Mashler set the paint can on the breakfast tray. The doll carriage was now really splendid. But the tray had a ring. There was nothing to do but paint it. In doing so, Mr. Mashler spattered paint all over the stove.

Mrs. Mashler had always wanted a silver stove top. She quickly brought other things that Mr.

Mashler could paint: the lamp base, the mirror frame, the old trash can, and the kitchen scales. In addition, Mr. Mashler painted the stovepipe, the curtain rod, the doorknob, and the teakettle.

"Do you think we might be overdoing it?" he asked, as he worked. But Mrs. Mashler couldn't see enough silver. Besides he had to paint everything that had been spattered.

"For instance, your nose," he said and raised his brush to Mrs. Mashler's face.

"Even better, your shoes," she squealed.

Mr. Mashler's shoes were covered with silver flecks. They were old, so it didn't matter. He took them off, and presto, they were silver. They were unrecognizable.

But the paint was all gone.

Mr. and Mrs. Mashler were breathless with laughter and had to sit down.

"What are you making so much noise for?" asked Julie, groping her way into the kitchen. Everywhere she looked she saw silver. In the middle of the room was the most beautiful doll carriage she had ever seen.

"Who is that for?" she asked.

"That's for you," said Mrs. Mashler.

"And who do the silver shoes belong to?" she asked.

"They belong to me," said Mr. Mashler.

But he couldn't make Julie believe that. Somehow someone had come and had brought the doll carriage. Everything he had touched had turned to silver. He had taken off his shoes so as not to disturb anyone, and then he had forgotten them.

"Well now, so far as I'm concerned, it could have happened that way," said Mrs. Mashler.

Next morning she sent Julie over to their neighbor. "Tell her your story. She'll enjoy it!"

Julie took the silver shoes with her as proof.

# The Christmas Roast

Once a man found a goose on the beach. The November storms had been raging several days before. She had probably swum too far out, been caught, and then tossed back to land again by the waves. No one in the area had geese. She was a real white domestic goose.

The man stuck her under his jacket and took her home to his wife. "Here's our Christmas roast."

They had never kept an animal and had no coop. The man built a little shed out of posts, boards, and roofing board right next to the house wall. The woman put sacks in it and put an old sweater on top of them. In the corner they put a pot with water in it.

"Do you know what geese eat?" she asked.

"No idea," said the man.

They tried potatoes and bread, but the goose

wouldn't touch anything. She didn't want any rice either, and she didn't want the rest of their Sunday cake.

"She's homesick for the other geese," said the woman.

The goose didn't resist when they carried her into the kitchen. She sat quietly under the table. The man and the woman squatted before her, trying to cheer her up.

"But we aren't geese," said the man. He sat on a chair and tried to find some band music on the radio. The woman sat beside him, her knitting needles going clickety-clack. It was very cozy. Suddenly the goose ate some rolled oats and a little cake.

"She's settling down, our lovely Christmas roast," said the man. By next morning the goose was waddling all over the place. She stuck her neck through the open doors, nibbled on the curtains, and made a little spot on the doormat.

The house in which the man and woman lived was a simple one. There was no indoor plumbing, only a pump. When the man pumped a bucket full of water, as he did every morning before going to work, the goose came along, climbed into the bucket, and bathed. The water spilled over, and the man had to pump again.

In the garden there was a little wooden house, which was the toilet. When the woman went to it, the goose ran behind her and pressed inside with her. Later she went with the woman to the baker and then to the dairy store.

When the man came home from work on his bicycle that afternoon, the woman and the goose were standing at the garden gate.

"Now she likes potatoes, too," reported the woman.

"Wonderful," said the man and stroked the goose on the head. "Then by Christmas she will be round and fat."

The shed was never used, for the goose stayed in the warm kitchen every night. She ate and ate. Sometimes the woman set her on the scales, and each time she was heavier.

When the man and the woman sat with the goose in the evening, they both imagined the most marvelous Christmas food.

"Roast goose and red cabbage. They go well

together," said the woman and stroked the goose on her lap.

The man would rather have had sauerkraut than red cabbage, but for him the most important thing was the dumplings. "They must be as big as my head and all the same size," he said.

"And made with raw potatoes," added his wife.

"No, with cooked ones," asserted the man. Then they agreed that half the dumplings should be made with raw potatoes and half with cooked ones. When they went to bed, the goose lay at the foot and warmed them.

All at once it was Christmas.

The wife decorated a small tree. The husband biked to the shop and bought everything they would need for the great feast. He also brought a kilo of extra-fine rolled oats.

"Even if it's her last," he said with a sigh, "she should at least know that it's Christmas."

"I've been wondering," began the woman, "how, do you think, should we . . . I mean . . . we still have to . . . ." But she couldn't get any farther.

The man didn't say anything for a while. "I can't do it," he said finally.

"I can't either," said the woman. "I could, if it were just any old goose. But not this one. No, I can't do it no matter what."

The man grabbed the goose and fastened her onto his baggage carrier. Then he rode his bicycle

to a neighbor's. In the meantime, the woman cooked red cabbage and made the dumplings, one just as big as the next.

The neighbor lived far away, to be sure, but still not so far that it was a day's journey. Nevertheless, the man did not come home until evening. The goose sat contentedly behind him.

"I never saw our neighbor. We just rode around," he said ashamedly.

"It doesn't matter," said the woman cheerfully.

"While you were gone, I thought it over and decided that adding something else to dinner would just spoil the good taste of the red cabbage and the dumplings."

The woman was right, and they had a good meal. At their feet the goose feasted on the extra-fine rolled oats. Later all three sat together on the sofa in the living room and enjoyed the candlelight.

The next year, for a change, the woman cooked sauerkraut to go with the dumplings. The year afterward there were broad noodles to go with the sauerkraut. They were such good things that nothing else was needed to go with them.

And so time passed. Goose grew very old.

# The Bird Feeder

When Mama opened the window in the morning to wake Jay, a load of snow fell from the window-sill onto the carpet. It had snowed during the night. The sparrows sat in the branches outside and scolded.

"He never built the bird feeder," said Jay reproachfully.

"We'll get him to do it today," answered Mama.

Papa sat contentedly at the breakfast table. It was Sunday, and he was looking forward to being lazy. He waited for Mama to butter a roll for him. Not that he couldn't have done it himself. But Papa liked to have Mama take over and was happy to let himself be waited on now and then.

Now, however, she had no desire to. Sometimes it pleased her that she was more capable than Papa, and she liked to show how well she did everything.

But she didn't like him to rely too much on her.

"Jay and I would be very glad if you would get around to building that bird feeder at last. It's winter, it has snowed, and the poor birds are hungry," she said.

"I can help you," said Jay.

Papa didn't move. He sat there and waited for Mama to butter a roll for him. But she didn't.

"Sunday is a day of rest," said Papa. "Why must I build a bird feeder on Sunday?"

"All fathers do," cried Jay.

"Bird feeders are men's things," said Mama. Really, she could have built it too. She could saw, hammer, drive nails, change blown fuses, and she understood a great deal about cars. But she didn't see why she should build a bird feeder while Papa stood beside her and watched. Perhaps even Jay could have built it, although Mama wasn't entirely sure he wouldn't hurt himself. Yet he could give Papa a hand, she thought.

Papa couldn't withstand both Mama and Jay. So he buttered his roll himself, reluctantly dragged himself out of his chair, and shuffled down cellar. Jay rushed after him.

Mama heard Papa say to Jay, "Let's build a snowman instead. I'm good at that."

And Jay answered, "We're building a bird feeder or nothing."

Mama was satisfied. Jay described exactly how the bird feeder should look. He knew what was needed and where everything was. Papa didn't know his way around the cellar very well. It was Mama's territory. She had collected fruit crates, which they could use now. In one corner she had put away some sheets of plastic, and on a hook hung a roll of wire. Somewhere there were posts that they would use to mend the fence in the spring. Jay brought everything together.

Papa stood around. He didn't know where the hammer was, he couldn't find a saw, there were no nails, and he very much hoped that without all those things he couldn't build a bird feeder. But Jay had already run upstairs. Mama had the tools in the kitchen cupboard and the nails in the pantry, for she liked to have everything handy. Jay dragged it all downstairs and took it to Papa. He described exactly what Papa should do, and Papa did each step just the way Jay told him to. First he sawed little boards from the fruit crates; they would become the floor. While doing so he caught his left thumb on the saw.

Mama bandaged it and said, "That's no reason to go right to bed. Go back to the cellar and get on with it!"

In the meantime, Jay had made the boards into a floor with a piece of molding. Now he showed Papa how the sticks for the roof should be fastened. First Papa nailed his thumb bandage firmly to the wood; then he hammered his forefinger. After he soaked it in a basin of cold water for half an hour, Mama shooed him back to the cellar. Jay had already set the roof on the posts and covered it with plastic. Papa only had to fasten it all around with wire. He took the pliers and with them promptly pinched himself on the ball of the thumb. Mama caught him as he was knotting a scarf for a sling to put his arm in. "It will keep you from finishing the bird feeder," she said and laid the scarf back in the drawer.

Papa crept into the cellar to annihilate the bird feeder, but Jay had finished it. It was crooked and rickety, to be sure, and it had also turned out to be somewhat small, but you could still tell what it was supposed to be. Papa and Jay set one of Mama's posts in the front yard and fastened the bird feeder on top of it. Then Mama strewed the crumbled Christmas cake from last year inside it, and the first sparrows began pecking at it at once. Papa and Jay sat at the window and watched how they scuffled and disappeared with the best crumbs into the shrubbery. Papa was very proud of his creation, and Mama praised him. It turned into a lovely Sunday.

The next morning Jay looked out at the bird feeder. There sat a fat black cat in it. Jay threw up the window and cried, "Hey, you, get out of there!" The cat tried, but she couldn't; she was stuck fast.

Her head and paws hung out in front, behind waved an excited tail.

Jay and Mama ran out. Mama called to Jay to be careful, for cats have sharp claws. She pushed from behind, and Jay coaxed from the front. "Now come on, jump!"

The cat went crazy and thrashed and struggled. The bird feeder wobbled on its post, and the roof lifted a little.

"As long as she stays so fat, she can't manage it," said Mama. "Perhaps when she gets hungry and loses weight. . . ."

The cat meowed. Suddenly Jay and Mama felt sorry for her. They got some sardines, and the cat ate politely out of the can Jay held up to her. The sparrows sat around on the branches and scolded.

"All right, we'll feed them too," said Mama. She strewed crumbs on the windowsill for them, and then they watched from the inside as the sparrows pecked at them.

The cat fell asleep in the feeder. Her paws hung down limply in front, and behind dangled the long tail. The sparrows had quickly figured out that she could do nothing to them. They grew bolder and

bolder. Some blustered around the roof; others flew within a hair of her nose. When a sparrow seized the cat's tail, it was too much. The cat hunched up, arched her back, strained against the boards, the molding, and the wire, and the bird feeder broke apart.

The cat made one spring and disappeared.

What else could Mama do but make Jay a new bird feeder, strong and solid? She really couldn't expect Papa to build it with his bandaged hand. He stood contentedly beside her and watched.

# The Tinsel Tree

Each year during the holidays, all the relatives were invited to Aunt Gertrude's house.

Aunt Gertrude was much more elegant than her relatives. She had a big house with many rooms full of carpets on the floor, pictures hanging on the wall, and overstuffed furniture in every corner.

Aunt Gertrude was always happy to hear people say how grand and fashionable everything was at her house. But at Christmas people had to admire her home even more.

When the relatives came, she stood in the doorway and cried, "First, look at my tree!"

And everyone went and marveled: "How magnificent!" "Gorgeous!" "Fantastic!" "Legendary!" "Incomparable!" "Can't take my eyes off it!"

The tree reached to the ceiling—and Aunt Gertrude's house had high ceilings. The tree was filled with countless stands of candles, and tinsel hung from every branch. Each strand was of the same length and placed at precisely the same distance from the next.

This year Uncle Otto had again needed five days to decorate the tinsel tree to suit Aunt Gertrude.

"And it's the biggest he could buy in the whole city," she said. "The only bigger one is in front of the City Hall, and it's crooked!"

"This one is perfectly straight," said an old uncle, and everyone agreed with him.

They took their places in the chairs. Uncle Otto climbed onto a stepladder and, after a long time, lighted all the candles. An unmarried cousin seated himself at the piano. A girl cousin turned the pages. Aunt Gertrude led the Christmas carols, and everyone else joined in. The children had to study at home beforehand. One after the other they came forward and recited a poem. Woe to anyone who got stuck! At the end they each made a bow or a curtsey and received a kiss from Aunt Gertrude. Everyone said, "How nice," and sat there and stared at the tree.

It was boring.

Finally Aunt Gertrude got up, and everyone else quickly sprang up. Uncle Otto extinguished the candles and opened the sliding doors behind the tree. Just behind it in the next room stood the

long coffee table. The relatives crowded around it, and Aunt Gertrude explained where each person should sit.

There was the famous crumb cake, which only she could make. Everyone said so when Aunt Gertrude kept asking if they had ever had such crumb cake anywhere else.

"Never," said the old uncle. "We only have this crumb cake at your house. No one makes it the way you do."

Everyone said that the coffee, too, was really remarkable, that they had never before seen such a tasteful tablecloth, and that they envied Aunt Gertrude's beautiful coffee cups.

"Yes, and my dress?" she asked.

They all could only roll their eyes, for they could find no more words. And they all were so terribly bored.

Two children were not bored, however. They were called Lottie and Martin. They had secretly crept under the table. At first they played that they lived in a cave. They sat completely still under the tablecloth, which reached to the carpet. Later they played that they were sparrows and picked up the crumb-cake crumbs, which were especially numerous under Uncle Otto's chair.

Next they played horse stall, for the many feet scraped back and forth and sometimes stamped like horses. They had to be nimble not to get trampled.

Grandmama had taken off her shoes, which they placed next to the unmarried cousin. Martin got kicked in the head by the girl cousin, who was pouring coffee for everyone. Lottie had to laugh at that. They crept all around and finally managed to get under the tree. The tinsel hung down so low that no one could see them.

The tree was screwed into an iron stand. Martin and Lottie were amazed at how thick the stem was.

"No one could tip that over," said Lottie and shook the stand, but the tree stood firm.

"If it did tip over, what would happen?" asked Martin.

"No one could tip that over," Lottie repeated.

Martin straightened himself a bit and pressed against the stem again farther up. He marveled at how easy it was to tip the big tree.

Aunt Gertrude was just handing around a sweet liqueur, which everyone praised. Then, very slowly, the tree sank and fell the whole length of the coffee table. Its tip reached right to Aunt Gertrude. The branches covered cups and plates, crumb cake and liqueur. Only the heads of the relatives protruded from the foliage, and everyone had a shining wig of tinsel. The scene looked really lovely, but this time no one said so.

Everyone sprang up and helped each other get untangled and tried to right the tree again. It was much harder than it had been to tip it over. But it wasn't boring anymore. Everyone had something to do. The relatives had to clear away the dishes, pick the pine needles out of the crumb cake, and comb the tinsel out of their hair.

Aunt Gertrude ran around and wailed, "It's a mystery how this could have happened. This is a tragedy!" Then she caught sight of Uncle Otto and cried, "For years I've wanted you to fasten the tree more securely. Now look at the terrible mess we have!"

Uncle Otto drove nails into the doorframe and guyed the tree firmly with string. But Aunt Gertrude didn't like that either.

All the relatives consoled her. They said wholeheartedly that they had never before had such a nice time at her house. Grandmama finally found her shoes and urged them all to go home. "See how pale Lottie and Martin are. They've had a fright. They were so good that we haven't noticed them at all the whole afternoon!"

# The Highway Christmas

Their having to spend Christmas Eve on the road was Papa's doing. Sometimes he got very angry and did impossible things. Later he was sorry, for he really was good-natured and peaceable.

This time he got angry at Grandma—Mama's mother, that is. Papa and Mama had moved in with her so that she wouldn't have to live alone. It was just after Grandpa died and a long time ago now. Since then Mama and Papa always said, "Grandma lives with us."

But Grandma always said, "You live with me."

Papa couldn't bear it when she said that. Mama just laughed and said, "Let her talk, and don't worry about it."

But why did Grandma have to start in on Christmas Eve, of all times? Papa was in the living room, standing on a ladder, decorating the tree. He had

just put the silver ornament on top when Grandma came in and asked, "Why is the tree behind the door?"

"Where else would it be?" responded Papa.

"In my house it has always stood to the left of the window," said Grandma.

"And now it's behind the door," answered Papa from the ladder.

"As long as you are living with me, you should do what I say," retorted Grandma. And then the argument began. They said this and they said that, and then when Mama came from the kitchen to interfere, they all talked at once.

Papa was very angry. He tore the ornaments off the tree and threw them back into the cartons.

"What are you doing?" cried Mama.

"Pack the presents, the Christmas cookies, some bedding, and the toothbrushes. We are going to spend Christmas somewhere else—someplace where we'll be welcome and can set up our tree where we want it."

He took the tree, ran outside with it, and tied it to the roof of the car. Nickel was playing with his friend in the yard.

"What are you doing?" he asked Papa.

"We're going on a trip. And as we're going to be away on Christmas, we need our tree!" cried Papa and disappeared into the house.

"Great!" said Nickel's friend. And Nickel was very proud of Papa, who did such impossible things sometimes.

Grandma ran after Papa and wailed, "I didn't mean it that way!" But he just pushed past her.

Mama cried, "Are you really serious?" But Papa had already rolled up the bedding in a blanket and stuffed it into the trunk. So Mama bundled up all the presents and packed some underwear and clothes. She got the cookies out of the kitchen, and Grandma brought a thermos with tea.

Then Mama dressed little Max warmly and fastened him into his car seat behind her. Nickel gave Grandma a kiss, waved—and they were off.

Papa was still angry and drove very fast. He spun the steering wheel hard so that their heads joggled. He braked so that they all jolted forward. He honked when other cars wouldn't make room for him.

Nickel liked that, and Maxie screamed with pleasure.

But Mama said, "Please drive carefully, or I'll get out."

Then Papa grew calmer.

Later Mama asked, "Where are we going, anyhow?"

Papa answered, "To my Aunt Louise. It will be better there than with your mother, you'll see."

Mama was embarrassed to go to Aunt Louise's just like that. After all, they were four people, it was Christmas, and Aunt Louise had no idea they were coming. Nevertheless, it was no good arguing with Papa.

After an hour they reached the city where Aunt Louise lived. They drove up to the house, and Papa got out to ring the bell. He rang once, then again and again, but no one opened the door.

In the house next door a woman called out the window, "There's no one home," and she told Papa that Aunt Louise had gone away because she didn't want to be alone at Christmas. If she had known that visitors were coming, she would certainly have stayed home and been very happy to see them.

"Very well," said Papa. "Many thanks and Merry Christmas." He started off again.

"Where are we going now?" Mama asked.

Papa had recollected that he had an old school friend in this city. Papa thought he would certainly be pleased if they turned up unexpectedly, for he always used to be ready for a party.

Mama was not so certain, but she said nothing.

Nickel shouted, "Goody, we're going to a party!" And Maxie screamed with delight.

Papa's friend was at home all right, but he wasn't especially ready for a party. He didn't even remember Papa at first and had to rack his brains for a while. He only remembered when he saw Nickel, for Nickel looked just the way Papa had long ago.

He invited them into his house, and because it was lunchtime, his wife brought a bowl of potato soup for each of them. Mama was able to change Maxie in the next room, and Nickel was able to go to the bathroom. Then Papa's friend said, "Certainly you must have a long journey ahead of you. We don't want to hold you up. Everyone has a lot

to do today. It was nice that you could visit us even for so short a time."

Papa didn't trust himself to say anything. So they all climbed into the car and drove on. The friend and his wife stood in front of their house and waved.

A cousin of Papa's lived not far away. He had a wife and three children and a farmhouse with lots of room. They used to go there often, but because the cousin was so like Papa, they had got

angry once at the same time and had quarreled.

"We should go to your cousin," said Mama now.

Papa looked uncomfortable, but he agreed that Mama's suggestion was a good one. He stayed in the car in front of the farmhouse and sent Mama into the house. Nickel wanted to go too, but Papa held him tightly.

When Mama came back, she said to Papa, "Drive on."

"Is he still mad at me?" asked Papa.

"No," answered Mama, "but he and the three children are in bed with the mumps. Nickel and Maxie haven't had them yet."

Papa was very quiet.

Mama made him stop at every guesthouse and ask for rooms. But they had no luck. Either they were closed or all the rooms were taken. Nickel and Maxie were hungry, and Mama gave them some Christmas cookies. Once Papa stopped, and they all stretched their legs.

When they were driving again, Nickel asked when they would ever get to have their presents. He wanted his very much.

"When we are there," said Mama.

"When will we be there?" asked Nickel.

Mama said to Papa, "Please, let's turn around."

And Papa did—he turned around. They drove through almost empty streets. It was dark. Maxie slept. Mama and Nickel sang Christmas carols. Then Nickel fell asleep too. Later they stopped once more, and Mama gave Papa some hot tea.

"Good you thought of that," he said.

"Grandma thought of it," said Mama.

When they got home, no lights were burning. Mama carried Maxie to bed, and Papa lugged Nickel. They didn't wake up.

While everyone was still asleep the next morning, Papa took the tree from the roof of the car, put it in the living room behind the door, and began to decorate it. When he was half finished, he moved it to the left of the window. Mama came and brought the presents. She carried Maxie into the room, and Nickel bounced along behind her. Papa lighted the candles.

"Now we are going to have Christmas at last!" cried Nickel.

But Papa said, "Wait a minute." He went to get Grandma, who had not yet appeared. He hugged her and gave her a kiss and cried, "Merry Christmas!"

Papa is usually the best and most peaceable of men.

"How glad I am that you are here again!" cried Grandma. "I do so like living with you. But," she added, "isn't it really better with the tree to the left of the window instead of behind the door?"

"Grandma!" cried Mama.

But Papa laughed.

# Trudie's Uncle

Mia said nothing to anyone about Trudie. Not anyone at home and not any one of the other children with whom she usually played. Like Mia, the other children all lived in the huge, new apartment houses: Freddie in Section A, on the second floor, Anders and Birgit in Section D, on the ground floor, and John in Section C, one floor under Mia. They all played together in the little playground.

Only Trudie didn't, for she lived on the other side of the street. For a long time she had stood on the curb on the other side and looked across. One day she simply ran across. The cars moving along the street in four lanes braked and honked, and many drivers rolled down their windows and scolded.

"She's dumb!" Anders and Jochen yelled.

Trudie had stood there and smiled, but she

wasn't asked to play with them. Then she ran away
again. Mia saw that she had lost a mitten and
picked it up. She just caught up with Trudie as
she was about to run across the street again.

"You have to go through the tunnel!" Mia
called.

"Will you come with me?" Trudie asked, and
Mia went.

The houses on the other side of the street were
old. They had towers with gates through which you
went into a courtyard. Behind the houses were more
courtyards and more houses. Trudie lived way in
back on the top floor. No one was in the apartment.
There was a baby carriage in the hallway. In the
kitchen was a bed and the TV set. In the living
room were two more beds. On one there was a
knitted coverlet and on it sat a doll with a silk dress
and long, black curls.

"How beautiful she is," whispered Mia.

"She's only for decoration and not to play with,"
said Trudie, "but you can hold her for a while."

She climbed onto a stool and got a glass dish
from the cupboard. In the kitchen she spooned out
preserved plums. "They grow in my uncle's garden," said Trudie.

Mia wanted to talk about Trudie at home, but Mama had no time. She had to shop, and Mia had to go along. In the supermarket there were dolls almost as beautiful as the one at Trudie's. They had curls and silk dresses too.

"I want a doll like that for Christmas," said Mia.

"But that's junk," said Mama.

So Mia didn't say anything about Trudie.

Now when Trudie stood on the other side of the street and waved, Mia ran along the street to the pedestrian tunnel. The other children didn't notice. So no one knew when Mia was with Trudie.

On the morning of Christmas Eve, Trudie asked, "Do you want to come to my uncle's? He'll give us something if we come."

Mia too had an uncle who always gave her something. He was Mama's youngest brother. When he visited, he romped around with Mia or he went with her wherever she wanted. Mia laughed herself sick over the stories he told.

Mia was very curious to know what Trudie's uncle was like.

They went along the street to the end. Then they crossed a few empty lots. A dog chased after them behind a wire fence, and Trudie teased it with a stick. Mia was afraid that the dog could jump over the fence with one spring, but Trudie laughed at her. Later they went on a path along a canal and turned into a hedged lane that led through allotment gardens with little sheds in them. Way at the end stood a little shack that was almost like a house. Trudie's uncle lived there.

The shutters were closed, and there was no smoke coming out of the pipe that stuck out of the wall.

"Perhaps he isn't there," said Mia.

But Trudie drummed on the shutters and banged on the door. She called and whistled.

"Hey," said a voice inside. "What's all the racket?"

"It's me," said Trudie.

The uncle opened the door. He had to bend, for he was very large. He was unshaven, and his trousers were dirty. Furthermore, he was in a bad mood.

"What are you doing here?" he growled.

"We came to wish you Merry Christmas," said Trudie and made a curtsey.

"Don't talk nonsense," said the uncle. He didn't want to believe that it really was Christmas Eve.

Mia thought that was very strange. The uncle told them to come into the shed. Trudie had to pump while he held his head under the water. He groaned and moaned. Then he plodded into the house ahead of them and fished a newspaper from under the table. He looked at the date and yelled, "You think I'm going to fall for your tricks! Here, today is the twenty-second!"

"Your paper is from the day before yesterday!" said Trudie.

The uncle tried to make a fire in the stove with cardboard and kindling, but it kept going out.

Trudie took a broom and swept all the bottles and cans that were lying about everywhere under the bed. So many were there already that she shoved some of them under the clothes cupboard.

Then she asked, "What are you giving me for Christmas?"

The uncle said, "First I have to be sure this isn't some rotten trick of yours."

He blew into the stove again, then pulled himself up, put on his jacket, and scolded because Trudie swept his boots under the bed with the bottles. He put on his fur cap, slammed the door behind

Trudie, Mia, and himself, and cried, "Come on, we'll go off to Kitty's."

They went along the lane back through the shantytown, then across a field and a factory area, across a street, and finally came to a low wooden building. Mia read, *Good Beer. Proprietress Kitty Reese.*

The barroom was thick with smoke and full of men who all knew the uncle. He shoved Trudie and Mia ahead of him and yelled, "These two want to make me believe that today is Christmas Eve. Want to bet they're kidding?"

"I'll take your bet!" called a couple of men. They proved to the uncle that it really was so, and because they all said it, finally he believed it. He had lost his bet and had to order a round of beer.

Trudie and Mia got some money for the vending machines and the jukebox. Trudie was familiar with everything, but for Mia it was all new.

In the next room they discovered a table-tennis game. And in the middle of it all Kitty brought them a bowl of pea soup. Later she came to them again and asked, "Don't you have to go home?"

Then Trudie and Mia noticed that it was dark

outside. They hurried into the barroom, and Trudie said to her uncle, "We're going now. Do I get a Christmas present?"

She got a ten-mark piece, and the uncle gave Mia a five-mark piece. They each had to give him a kiss, which was prickly and didn't smell very good. Mia was glad when they were outside in the air.

Trudie thought they should now go to the right. Mia thought that the way they had come was to the left, but she went along with Trudie. There was no one on the street, and only a few lights were burning. Trudie went left again, but soon they realized that both turns were wrong.

Trudie said, "We'll go back and begin all over again."

But they couldn't find Kitty's anymore. They tried this direction and that one, and soon they realized that they were really lost.

Trudie said, "Damn it!" and much worse words. Mia agreed with her.

Finally they met three men who were probably coming home from the late shift. They told them where they lived and asked how they could get there. But the men didn't know either and were in a hurry to get home.

On a corner they saw a telephone booth. Mia's parents had a telephone, and Mia knew the number, too, but they had no change. Trudie had the ten-mark piece. Mia had the five-mark piece.

Across the way there was a house. Trudie and Mia ran to it. They rang the bell, and someone called, "Who's there?" For a while they heard nothing more. Finally a big boy opened the door.

"Can you make change? We want to telephone," said Mia and held out the five-mark piece to him.

"Wait a minute," said the boy, took the money, and closed the door. They waited a long time.

When no one opened again, they rang a few more times. Then a woman flung open the door and screamed, "Can't a person have any peace on Christmas?" She turned around and said to someone inside, "I thought you chased them away?"

"I did," said the boy.

Trudie said quickly, "He took our money!"

"Liar," cried the boy.

"Impudence," said the woman and slammed the door.

Trudie and Mia ran away from there as fast as they could. They ran until Mia had a stitch in her side. Now they were in a street on which cars were driving. Trudie stood on the curb and raised her thumb.

"What are you doing?" asked Mia.

"Hitching," said Trudie.

A car stopped beside them, and Mia saw that it was a taxi.

"Is this a joke or do you want a ride?" asked the driver.

"Of course we want a ride," said Trudie and climbed into the back of the car.

The driver asked again, "Can you pay? That's what I want to know."

Trudie dangled the ten-mark piece under his nose. Then Mia climbed in and gave her address. They were at the new apartment houses very quickly, and the fare came to nine marks thirty.

"Just right," said Trudie, and she handed over the money. Then she ran quickly across the street; luckily no cars were passing at the moment. Still, the taxi, which had turned around, had to brake. The driver honked and yelled at her.

Mia ran home too. What excitement she found there! Papa had gone to look for Mia and had just come back. Mama had called the police, and a policeman had asked all the children where Mia could be. No one had any idea that Mia was with Trudie, and they were worried. But now that was past, and they could celebrate Christmas.

Later Mia told them all about everything.

Papa looked at Mama and Mama looked at Papa.

Mia was afraid they would forbid her to play with Trudie. But Mama said, "I would like very much to meet Trudie."

# Brandied Gingerbread

"Once," said Ella, who cleaned for us, "once my three brothers and I almost became orphans at Christmastime—without a father and mother, alone in the world. That was a long time ago, and this is how it happened.

"In our village in Lower Saxony they used to make a special Christmas delicacy. A week before, they baked a huge quantity of gingerbread on a cookie sheet. One half was cut in squares, iced with sugar, and put by for us children. The other half they put into a big stone crock, the way you do pickles or sauerkraut. Then they poured brandy over it until the crock was full. It was covered up and put away somewhere cool. At Christmas they brought it to the table. The gingerbread was ladled into deep soup plates and eaten with spoons. There was bread and knackwurst with it. Of course it was only for the grown-ups, but we children could taste it. Everyone got very red in the face from eating it and became very loud and cheerful.

"So—this particular year Mother had filled the crock and covered it. Our house was small and had no cellar. Mother didn't know where to put the crock, and finally she stored it in the bedroom on the press, which is what we used to call a small clothes cupboard in those days.

"In the night our father woke up because the dog had barked. Perhaps the dog had been chasing a cat or an owl had flown too close to his nose. He wouldn't calm down, and when he was finally quiet, Father couldn't get to sleep again. He lay there thinking, considering how much there was still to do before Christmas and looking forward to the good brandied gingerbread. Then it occurred to him that the crock was nearby. He decided to try it once, just to see if Mother had got the mixture right. Too much gingerbread was really not good; on the other hand, too much brandy didn't hurt.

"So as not to wake Mother, Father climbed carefully out of bed, pulled the stool over to the press, moved his jacket and trousers from the stool to the windowsill, and climbed up. He fished for the cover, lifted it, and plunged his other hand into the crock, for of course he had no spoon. He slurped out of his cupped hand and decided that Mother had done her work well.

"He climbed down off the stool and cautiously lowered himself into bed. In those days we slept on mattresses filled with straw that rustled at the slightest movement. Still, Father was so quiet that Mother only gave a little snort once and slept right on. He had grown comfortably warm in the stomach, and he fell asleep.

"Soon afterward the dog barked again—this time only a short yelp, the way dogs do when they're dreaming. But Father started up and lay awake again. He brooded a little and then thought, It should be all right. Or perhaps he didn't think anything. In any case, he climbed up on the stool again and scooped out some of the mixture. Mother turned, but she didn't wake up. In addition to a warm belly, Father now had a hot face. He was tired, to be sure, but he decided to go into the crock once more, because if he went to sleep right off, he wouldn't have another chance. Also, if he had some more, he would be sure to sleep afterward.

"When he lay down again, the bed seemed to be swinging and sometimes it seemed to fly and land upside down. From experience Father knew a good remedy for that. He put one foot firmly on the floor. Immediately the bed stood still. But now Father's foot was slowly growing cold.

"It was cold outside, and the chill came in through the chinks in the window. In the evenings Mother would always put a fieldstone in the oven. When the stone grew hot, she wrapped it in her apron and put it at the foot of the bed. Father usually laughed at her, for he never had cold feet. Now he would gladly have shared the fieldstone with Mother. But he didn't dare, for usually Mother slept lightly and wakened instantly. He said to himself, 'The gingerbread has warmed my face and my stomach. Now it will have to do something for my cold feet.'

"It wasn't as easy for him to climb on the stool as it had been before; it reeled just like the bed. Father braced himself on the windowsill with his other foot until the stool had quieted. He had to

feel with both hands before he found the gingerbread crock. When he finally captured it, the lid
clattered to the floor, making a considerable racket.
Mother sat up and cried, 'What's that?'

"Father started, one foot slipped from the windowsill, the other from the stool, and he crashed
against the bedpost. He hit his back and got a lot
of black-and-blue marks. The crock fell with him,
and it landed within an inch of Mother's head on
the straw mattress.

"Yes, that's really what happened," said Ella.
"It turned out very well, considering. Father could
have broken his neck, and the stone crock missed
killing our mother by a hair. Then we would have
been orphans. So the only misfortune was that
Father got no brandied gingerbread for Christmas;
it had all run into the mattress. Mother dumped it
on the manure heap, and she stuffed a new mattress
in the barn. Our chickens were staggering around
the barnyard all day long.

"Mother didn't speak a single word to Father
until New Year's. He hobbled around the village
and told everyone he had bad rheumatism.

"Every year afterward, Mother left the crock of
gingerbread in a neighbor's cellar until Christmas."

# Television in the Snow

By afternoon Mama had had enough. Early in the morning she had gone to the city. With lots of other people she had crowded into the department stores, all Christmas-decorated, and had bought presents. Later, in the bus, her shopping bag had torn, and by the time she got home her arms were nearly paralyzed from carrying all the packages. At noon she had frozen her fingers washing the windows. Then, after she got the Christmas cookies into the oven, someone telephoned, and all the cookies were burned. Then, while she was washing the dishes, she dropped the lid to the coffeepot, so now she couldn't use the pot anymore. She'd had enough; she wanted to rest awhile.

Just about that time the children's program began on the television. Mama heard the TV babbling and screaming and Melanie and Peter laughing loudly with delight.

"Please go outside for a while. You haven't had any fresh air today," Mama cried. Melanie and Peter were cross, but she wouldn't listen to their arguments. She shoved them both out the door, turned off the television, and lay down.

Peter and Melanie stood out in the courtyard. It was cold and wet, for it had snowed a few days before. The janitor had shoveled the snow into huge piles, which were now gray and dirty. His shovel was still there. Angrily Peter took the handle and rammed holes in the snow, one after the other.

"Oh, I'm mad!" he screamed.

"But I'm even madder," cried Melanie and kicked the snow pile.

"What makes you so angry?" asked the janitor.

"Mama turned off the television and sent us out-side, just because she wants to rest," cried Peter and Melanie.

"If you always yell like that, I can understand why," said the janitor. "And so you're making television for yourselves?" He gestured toward the holes.

"What do you mean?" asked Peter and Melanie.

"Well, if you want to, you can look way down in the holes and see a different program in each.

Naturally it isn't as clear as on an ordinary set, but if you try, you can see it."

"I don't believe that," said Peter.

The janitor bent way over a hole in the snow. "Well, in this one here . . . there's a cowboy movie on—fantastic! The horses are galloping so fast it's scary. . . . There! I thought the little fat one would fall off. He's just about broken his neck!"

Melanie sat beside him. "But I don't see anything at all!"

The janitor stood up and pushed Melanie so that her nose almost went into the hole. "Just look in! It's way down and pretty small, but you can make it out."

"Is that so?" asked Peter.

"I don't know," said Melanie. "I think so."

"But Melanie," said the janitor. "You see how the cowboys are dismounting and making a campfire. And there—on the hill to the left—an Indian has just appeared."

"I see him, I see him!" screamed Melanie.

"Let me look now," cried Peter and shoved Melanie to one side.

"Come here," said the janitor. He dragged Peter

by the collar to another hole. "You get the next channel. Lean close to it and pay attention. It will take awhile before you can make anything out, just like the other television. Now, is the picture there yet?"

"Not yet," said Peter, disappointed.

"Make an effort. You aren't any less intelligent than Melanie. As far as I know, there is a cartoon on now about a duck who can't swim. She keeps on trying, but she goes under like a stone."

"Can you see it?" asked Melanie.

"Yes," answered Peter. "The duck is so dumb that she can't get her wings to work right and keeps falling on her beak. Lucky she can walk at least!"

"Please, please let me see the duck," cried Melanie.

But Peter wouldn't let her. Then Melanie squatted in front of another snow hole and said, "Then you can't look either and see how our car broke down on vacation and how everyone was so shaken up and I had to drive."

"So what!" cried Peter. "I have a hole with the moon landing. And who gets to set foot on the moon first? Me! I'm the one!"

"I don't care," replied Melanie, for she was watching a wonderful film in which she played the leading role.

Peter and Melanie kept poking new holes in the snow with the shovel handle and sticking their

heads in. Above them Mama opened the window and called down, "Peter, Melanie, get up at once. You are soaked through! Come up before you catch cold!"

They had to put on warm slippers, and Mama said, "If you want, you can watch television now." But they didn't want to anymore. Instead, they looked out the window.

Down below stood the janitor. He bent over one of the holes, looked for a long time, then shook his head, and walked away.

"What do you suppose he saw?" asked Melanie.

# The Travel Story

Once there was a boy who didn't celebrate Christmas until May. The boy was named George.

George's parents had quarreled for such a long time that they could no longer live with each other. They now had two houses. Each wanted to have George live with them, but George liked Papa just as much as Mama. So he alternated, a few weeks in one place and a few weeks in the other. This particular year he had celebrated his birthday with Mama. Now he was going to spend Christmas with Papa. Two weeks beforehand, Mama packed his things. She gave him her presents, and he was allowed to unwrap everything right then. Then she called a taxi, gave the driver Papa's address, and ran back into the house before George could wave. Mama was often quite peculiar now.

Papa said to George, "Why should we both sit

here alone and celebrate Christmas? I've planned something else. We'll travel!"

George thought that was great.

At the travel agent's Papa booked passage for two people to Africa. George called Mama from the airport. He said good-bye and asked if Mama would think of him at Christmas. Yes, she would, and she promised very definitely to send him a greeting: "You'll hear from me."

George flew to Africa with Papa.

They had a beautiful hotel room. From one window they could see the Mediterranean; from the other they could see palm trees. It was warm, and they went swimming in the pool right away. Then they went to the harbor, dawdled through the alleyways, and ran on the beach.

They bought sandals and straw hats. That night George was allowed to stay up as late as Papa. They sat at a little table along the edge of the sidewalk and watched the many exotic people.

"Do you like it?" asked Papa.

George liked it.

After a few days Papa said, "Today is Christmas Eve."

George hadn't been thinking about it. It was like summer here, and nothing had reminded him of Christmas. Most of all there were no Christmas trees here. Papa had not been able to find even a branch.

They sat in the hotel room. George got a colored shirt from Papa, and he gave him a huge mussel shell he had found on the beach. Papa could use it for an ashtray.

George thought about Mama a great deal. She had promised a greeting, but she had not been heard from. Perhaps she had called. George wanted to ask downstairs, but he didn't know the language.

Papa suggested, "Let's go for a walk."

There were big crowds on the streets. It was like any other night, no different. George and Papa ate something; then they went to the harbor. A ship was just leaving. It was brightly lighted and had strings of colored lights on all the masts.

George wanted to go back to the hotel. But Mama still had not called. Nothing came from her the next day and not the day after either.

George was disappointed and angry. "That

wasn't a real Christmas celebration. I don't like Mama anymore. She forgot me."

Papa said nothing.

When they were home again, George remained with Papa. Papa told Mama about the decision on the telephone and said it wasn't his fault. Mama wanted to speak with George, but he refused. Then she hung up.

In May the mailman brought a package for George. It was dented and the paper was torn. Three-ply string held it together. On the front were many marks and stampmarks, and on top there was something in writing that no one could decipher. The package was very light.

George shook it and heard how it crackled and

rustled inside. "Perhaps there are mice in there," he said.

Papa looked at the address carefully and said, "Open it up!"

George cut the string and pulled off the paper. Inside was a little package tied up with ribbon. George took it off and lifted the cover. Underneath there was colored tissue paper. He pulled it apart and found nothing but dried, withered twigs and a little heap of pine needles in a corner.

But there was a letter, too:

Dear George:

Here is a Christmas tree for you, because surely there won't be any in Africa. Greetings to Papa. Think of me. I'm thinking of you both.

Mama

Papa said to George, "Mama didn't forget you at Christmas. The mail was so slow that we were already gone when the package reached Africa. Since then it has followed us back here and gone astray a few times on the way."

George called Mama right away to tell her everything.

Then Papa and Mama had a long conversation. That afternoon she came. On the table was the dried-up pine tree, which hadn't a single needle left.

George cried, "Now we can really celebrate Christmas!"

Papa and Mama didn't quarrel at all.

That night George went with Mama again for the next few weeks. But soon Papa came to visit.

Perhaps Mama and Papa will get together again too.

# Curiosity

A man who was himself very curious had a curious wife. That wasn't so bad, except that at Christmastime they got on each other's nerves a bit. They had a small apartment: a living room, a kitchen, bath, and a tiny hallway; there weren't many places in it to hide Christmas presents from each other. Each knew that the other was almost bursting with curiosity and had already searched for the presents.

Once, when the man came home from work, he surprised his wife with all his clothes out of his closet and all his shirts out of his drawer.

"Oh," she said and blushed, "I only wanted to put everything in order." And she stuffed everything back into the closet and the drawer. But the husband knew that she had been looking for her Christmas present.

When the woman came home from shopping,

she found her husband under the bed. "I wanted to clean a little," he said, and his ears grew red.

"With your hands?" asked the wife. She knew that he had been looking to see where she had hidden his present.

They hardly talked except to say, "What are you giving me? Please, tell me, I'm going to burst!"

As much as they wanted to know what they were getting, they were equally closemouthed about what they were giving. Each took great pains to find a hiding place in the little apartment that the other couldn't discover ahead of time.

When the early morning of Christmas Eve finally came, they couldn't wait any longer. The wife said they should have their presents, and then the whole day would be Christmas. That was all right with the husband; he didn't see why they should wait until evening. So they got up to get their presents.

The husband went into the living room; the wife ran into the kitchen. In the hallway they almost ran into each other, for the wife wanted to go into the living room and the man into the bathroom. Then they bumped into each other because the husband ran into the kitchen, and the wife did too. They ran here and there and sometimes called out, "We'll have it in a minute!"

But it took a long time. They had hidden the presents so well that they couldn't find them themselves anymore.

The husband pulled the cupboard away from the wall; the wife pulled the mattress off the bed frame. He unscrewed the lightbulbs; she rolled up the carpet. He took the back of the radio off; she looked along the tops of the draperies.

"I can't find it!" she finally cried.

"Look some more. I'm so curious about it," said the husband and stuck his head in the oven.

"As I am about yours," answered the wife. "Where do you have it?"

"If you hadn't kept looking for it all the time, I wouldn't have had to hide it so well," cried the husband. "It's your fault."

"And it's your fault that I can't find my present anymore!" she retorted. But because it was Christmas they didn't want to quarrel. Instead they kept searching together. Finally all the cupboards were emptied, all canisters and pots upside down, coat pockets turned inside out, and the pictures taken from the walls. They had looked everywhere three times over, and they had found nothing.

"Then at least tell me what it is," said the wife.

But the husband didn't want to. "Then it won't be a surprise anymore."

"Tell me what it looks like!" she wheedled. "Small, large, pointed, or round?"

"Small," said the husband. "And your present?"

"Pointed," said the wife.

Evening came. The apartment was completely torn apart. They wanted to turn on the lights and the bulbs had been removed. They wanted to get dinner and couldn't find the plates. They wanted to go to bed and had to look for the pillows.

"I can't take any more," cried the man and let himself fall into a chair. But because it was upside down, he jumped up again immediately. He turned it over and pricked his hand as he did, for something sharp in the upholstery had stabbed him. "Ow!" he yelled and took his handkerchief out of his pocket to wrap around his finger. As he did so, something small rolled out of his pocket onto the floor.

Had they found the presents at last? Who can say!

And what were they? That is their business— who would be so curious!

# The Tramp

Anne's father was a salesman. He traveled with his car and came home only on weekends. When he was there, he spent a lot of time with Anne and played and joked with her. Both were sad when he had to leave again early Monday morning. Anne had a calendar, and Papa had a notebook. Both counted and crossed off the days till Christmas. They were looking forward to the holidays and to a whole week of vacation besides.

But a week or two beforehand Papa said that it wasn't going to work; he had so much to do that all his accounts would be left for him to finish up. He was going to have to work right up until Christmas, and immediately afterward he would have to start traveling again. Anne heard him talking to Mama about it.

"It's all going to fall through again," he was saying.

"Just don't do it and stay with us," cried Anne.

Mama had a better idea. She would travel with Papa for a week; together they could make sure that Papa had some days free at Christmas.

"But who will stay with Anne?" asked Papa. "We can't leave her here in the house alone."

"I'll ask Aunt Erna about it," Mama decided.

Anne made a face, but she understood Mama was right.

Mama called up Aunt Erna. Yes, she said, of course it was an unusual situation; of course Aunt Erna was right that a woman belonged at home and not in the car if a child had a father who was never there; certainly she understood what Aunt Erna said, a child needed her mother, but she was lucky if she at least had an Aunt Erna; quite so. "Thank you very much for agreeing to come," said Mama, and then she hung up the phone.

Aunt Erna was a little old-fashioned, but Papa and Mama were happy that they could call her up and ask a favor. They said that Anne should be good and obedient.

The next morning Aunt Erna came, and Papa and Mama drove away.

Anne and Aunt Erna got along well, even if Aunt

Erna thought that Anne's hair would fall into the soup and braided it into pigtails for her. Anne was allowed to help Aunt Erna with the crossword puzzle, and Aunt Erna watched the children's programs on television with Anne.

It gets dark early around Christmastime. Aunt Erna rolled down all the shades, locked the front door, and put the chain on. She put a chair under the latch on the door to the balcony. In the cellar she shoved a basket of potatoes against the outside door.

"Now it's dark we don't want to have any more visitors," she said. "No one would come at this hour without calling first, outside of burglars."

"Or robbers," said Anne.

"That's almost the same thing," said Aunt Erna.

"Murderers too?" asked Anne.

"Don't speak of the devil!" cried Aunt Erna. She ran through the whole house, looked under all the beds, peered in the cupboards and behind all the doors. Yes, she even pulled out all the drawers in the bureau, into which only dwarf burglars could have fitted.

Anne ran behind her. She looked in the refrigerator and under the carpet.

Then Aunt Erna sat and listened. She said Anne shouldn't talk so loud; they couldn't hear if someone were sneaking about the house. Suddenly the telephone rang.

"My heart!" cried Aunt Erna.

But Anne knew that it was Papa and Mama, for they had promised to call in the evening. She lifted the receiver and asked how they were. Mama said she had accomplished a lot and it was a good thing she had gone. Anne said they were fine too.

By then Aunt Erna had pulled herself together and could come to the telephone. "Everything's been all right up till now!" she said.

"And why not?" said Mama. "Take care of yourselves until Saturday. We won't call again."

Next evening nothing happened. Then on the following evening, when Aunt Erna had closed and bolted everything up tight and had looked all over the house, in every corner and under all the furniture, the doorbell rang. Aunt Erna grabbed Anne by the arm and pulled her behind the corner of the kitchen stove. "Be very still. We are not at home," she whispered.

"But we *are* here," whispered Anne. "If you're afraid, I can open the door."

"Don't you dare!" Aunt Erna hissed.

The bell rang again. Aunt Erna grasped her arm so tightly that Anne cried, "Ow!"

It rang again and again. Then something banged against the door.

"They are breaking in," Aunt Erna whimpered. "I'll call the police!"

Bent down, she slipped through the hallway to the telephone. Anne flitted behind her. In the front door there was a little, round glassed peephole. Anne stood on tiptoe, but she couldn't see anything. Yes, from the side she saw something red shimmering, a piece of nose, a little beard. She turned to Aunt Erna and whispered, "I think it's a Santa."

Aunt Erna was hurriedly turning pages in the telephone book and responded softly, "Don't believe it. He wants to trick us. Take your hand off the doorknob!" For Anne wanted to open the door. Aunt Erna hurried over and grabbed her firmly.

Outside a voice said, "Now open up. I know you're there. You don't have to be afraid when Santa comes."

Anne knew that Santa was neither a burglar nor

a robber. The one last year was the father of Anne's
friend, and the one the year before was a neighbor.

Aunt Erna called, "Take yourself off immediately, or I shall call the police!"

"But Aunt Erna," said the Santa outside, "why
are you so hard on me? I came through snow and
ice—"

"Ha," cried Aunt Erna, "lying already. No snow,
no ice. It's warm and it's raining."

"Ahchoo," sneezed Santa.

"*Gesundheit!*" cried Anne.

"At least you are nice to me," said the visitor at the door. "Let me in, Anne. I want to give you something."

"No! That she will not do!" called Aunt Erna. "I know this trick from the newspapers. Someone disguises himself and overpowers helpless women and children! We won't fall for that."

Anne thought she heard the Santa laugh, but perhaps she didn't hear right. Anyway, he said then, "I'll tell you what. You leave the chain on but open the door a little crack so that I can pass my presents through to you."

"Not even that," said Aunt Erna.

"All right then. It's your hard luck," he said. Anne and Aunt Erna heard him walk away. Aunt Erna scolded him, but Anne was sulky, for she had very much wanted to open the door to Santa. But then she had promised Papa and Mama to be obedient.

Next morning, when Anne brought in the paper for Aunt Erna, she found two packages on the doorstep. They were wet and squishy from rain. Anne laid them on the breakfast table beside Aunt Erna. On one it said "For Anne," on the other "For Aunt Erna."

"The Santa left them," said Anne.

"Don't touch them!" cried Aunt Erna. "I know from the newspaper that the harmless-looking little packages they leave by the door are bombs!"

She grabbed up the fireplace shovel, carefully laid both packages on it, and carried them out into the yard. There she threw them under a bush.

"So," she said, satisfied, "now they can all blow

sky-high." But then she ran into the house as fast as she could.

Later Anne sneaked out and brought the packages to her room. In the one with her name on it were some sticky candies and a stuffed cat with a soaked behind. In the other, the one that was supposed to be for Aunt Erna, was a pretty handkerchief with an embroidered corner. Anne dried it on the radiator and gave it to Aunt Erna when she came down to lunch.

"How thoughtful of you," said Aunt Erna. She didn't ask where Anne got the hanky.

At the end of the week, Papa and Mama came home. Mama was very proud of how efficient they'd been. If she could travel with Papa for one more week, they could have a nice long Christmas holiday. Naturally it would depend on whether Aunt Erna could stay that much longer. Aunt Erna said yes, if there weren't more upsetting occurrences like what happened the other night when the Santa wanted to get in. And then she told the whole story.

"It was a tramp," she said, "with gigantic claws, a stubbled chin, and piercing eyes." Anne was surprised to hear Aunt Erna describe him so precisely, for she had never looked at him through the peep-hole. Papa and Mama laughed.

Later Anne lay in bed and heard Papa talking with a colleague on the phone. He discussed all kinds of business matters, and then he said, "She thinks you look like a tramp!"

# Special Effects

At Christmastime our church in the village is jam-packed. People who are never seen there the whole year through go then. Some send their children an hour ahead of time to get good seats and hold them. In the old days the men sat in the choir loft and the women in the nave. Now you can sit wherever you want to. You only have to be careful not to sit behind the columns where you can't see well.

Everything is very festive and impressive. Near the altar there is always a Christmas tree with many electric candles. The trumpet choir is stationed up in front and plays a prelude. It sounds a little sour; they say that comes from the cold, but it is no different in summer. Next the men's choral society sings, and the organ plays almost the whole time.

Our new minister wanted to have everything even more impressive and more festive. So after the ser-

mon he said, "And now, dear people, listen carefully. We will all—men, women, and children—
sing the hymn 'From Heaven Above.' The organ
will play one stanza, the next one we will sing alone,
next the organ, and so on. Do you all understand?"

Yes, we supposed so. The organ was already into
the elaborate introduction, through which we could
distinguish the melody. We didn't know for sure
if it was already supposed to be the first stanza or
if it was just the introduction. And besides, should
we sing the words to the first verse or the second?
We waited to see what the minister did. The organ
was silent, and we were silent too. The minister
sang alone. He had a beautiful, loud voice. When
he saw that we were hesitating, he raised his hands
as if to baptize an invisible baby—or so it looked,
at least. We sang, always a little behind him so we
didn't have to look in the hymnal but just listen to
his words. Aha, he was singing the first verse with
us. Then the organ began again. Unfortunately, a
couple of people who hadn't paid attention kept on
singing and stopped only after the minister wag-
gled his hands.

Now the surprise that would make everything even more impressive and festive was supposed to come. Shortly before the service the new minister had said to Fritz Willey, "You go into the sacristy, to the switch box. When you hear us singing the first stanza of 'From Heaven Above,' turn off the lights over the entrance. At the second verse turn the lights out in the right aisle, at the third those on the left. Then come both sides of the choir loft, in order, and finally the three big lights in the center aisle, one after the other. We will be singing the last verse by the light of the candles on the Christmas tree. Is that clear?"

The minister had thought the display out well, and if it had worked, we would certainly have been very impressed. Unfortunately, Fritz Willey had never been in the sacristy before. After the minister had gone, he looked around it for the first time. He found the switch box quickly, but there were so many levers and buttons that he didn't know which of them was for which light. He couldn't see out of the sacristy into the church or try them beforehand; he could only hear. He heard the trumpet choir, the men's choral society, the sermon, and the organ.

Then he heard us begin to sing. He figured that the button for the entrance light must be somewhere in the middle and pressed the middle switch on the bottom. It was for the lights in the sacristy, and all at once Fritz was in the dark. After he had calmed himself a little and he was lucky enough to turn the light on again, he heard that we had already begun the second verse. Quickly he pressed a switch somewhat higher, and the light on the right side of the choir loft went out.

August Lutge bellowed loudly, *"Liiiights* on," then clapped his hand over his mouth in horror; he had forgotten that he was in church and not at the bowling alley. Still, Fritz Willey had heard his shout, and the light in the choir loft went on again. Our verse was finished, and the organ began again. We had paid no attention when the light in the choir loft went off for a minute and then back on.

But when suddenly the three big lights in the middle aisle went out, we all looked up, the minister too. With raised faces we sang the third verse. We were still at it when the lights went on again; now the lights in both side aisles went out.

On the left aisle, at the end of a row, sat our

master electrician, Johann Bossey. He had watched the changing lights with concern, for no one could tell as well as he could that some repairs were going to be necessary within the next few days. During the joyful organ music that followed our singing, he stood up and pushed his way down the row. He caused some disturbance but no more than there was in the choir loft, which now lay in darkness, though the side aisles were illuminated again.

We sang and watched Johann Bossey as he hastened down the center aisle. He will soon find the trouble, we thought. For a second the light was completely gone and only streamed out from the Christmas tree; then all the lights that could be lighted went on.

The minister clattered down from the pulpit and hurried after the electrician. They disappeared behind the door to the sacristy.

We missed the minister badly. Since he wasn't singing away up front, we had to use the hymnals. We mixed up the words terribly; some people were singing the fourth verse while others were on the fifth and sixth. Still, we managed and the organ cut in with its music again.

Next the candles on the Christmas tree flickered on and off three times in quick succession and went out. Then the whole church lay in darkness. The organ made an ever-deepening whistling noise; we had been so proud when electric bellows had been installed last summer.

In the sacristy, Fritz Willey, assisted by the electrician and the minister, had produced a short circuit.

Luckily Johann Bossey knew the switch box very well, even in the dark. It wasn't the first time he'd stood there. He found the fuses and the lights went on everywhere again. The organ whistled like a locomotive before it began a new interlude. The preacher stood in the pulpit again, and we gathered breath to sing the last verse. Then the bells boomed out. In the sacristy, Fritz Willey had stumbled and grabbed the lever for the peal. For us it was a sign that the service was over, and we crowded excitedly toward the exit. We didn't even notice that the electrician had now extinguished the lights in the proper order until only the Christmas tree was glowing.

We went home as if we had come from the movie theater.

# The Keys

John and Jonas had lived on the second floor with their parents for some time. Mr. Grasmann lived all alone on the first floor, and the house belonged to him. He was pretty old. His wife was dead and his children had moved away. He didn't like people very much. He liked his dog and his dog liked him.

Mr. Grasmann complained automatically if John and Jonas romped over his head. Then Mama had words with him, and for a while they did not speak to Mr. Grasmann. But he complained about Mama too. She always left the front gate open when she came home from shopping. Mr. Grasmann implored her not to, but all the same she would forget again. Even Papa had trouble with Mr. Grasmann once. He had left his car parked in front of the house, and Mr. Grasmann wanted Papa to park it a little farther along. That parking place was his, and, after all, the house belonged to him. Papa said that anyone could use the street; it had nothing to do with the house. After he drove away, Mr. Grasmann put a big garbage can in the space. He got a ticket from the police, and Papa was glad that his car was parked around the corner.

It wasn't easy living with Mr. Grasmann. But his dog was even worse. He growled at everyone. They all made a wide circuit around him.

"Nevertheless," said Mama, "I'm sorry for Mr. Grasmann. After all, he's alone all day long. What will he do for Christmas? Will he go to see his children?"

Papa answered, "I wouldn't give it a thought."

"I'm only considering," replied Mama, "whether we should invite him here."

"No!" cried John. "We certainly shouldn't."

"No!" cried Jonas. "He can celebrate with his dog."

"You're mean," said Mama. But Papa said they weren't obligated to worry about Mr. Grasmann.

On Christmas Eve John and Jonas trimmed the tree with Papa. Then Mama wanted everyone to rest for an hour after the midday meal. But John and Jonas couldn't be still. They were much too excited about what was going to happen later. Mama gave them some milk and cookies, then sent them both outside the apartment; she wanted to get the presents ready with Papa. In the hallway John and Jonas listened to quick steps, bangs, scrapes, and rustling inside.

They stood at the window on the staircase. Through the branches of the trees they could see other houses. Candles were showing almost everywhere now. From where they were they couldn't see much, but from the street they would be able to see into the houses much better. They only needed to climb up on branches or pull themselves up on the windowsills.

At home Mama opened the door and said, "All right, it's ready!" But John and Jonas weren't there. She looked everywhere, but she didn't want to call down the stairs too loudly. That would disturb Mr. Grasmann and cause a row. Instead she ran downstairs and looked outside. Of course she left the front gate open again.

Five or six houses along she found John and Jonas. They were standing on a garbage can and looking into someone's window. Mama wanted to scold them, but she reminded herself that it was Christmas. She pulled them both down, and all three ran home.

Papa met them on the way. "Where were you?" he asked.

"We're just coming," they cried, breathlessly. They ran up the stairs to the door, which had slammed shut.

"Open it quickly!" cried John.

"We can't wait!" cried Jonas.

"Open it," said Mama to Papa.

"You open it," said Papa to Mama.

Then they realized that no one had taken a key. They couldn't get into the apartment. They were locked out. "And it had to happen at Christmas!" wailed Mama.

Papa rattled the doorknob. Then he stepped back a few steps. "Out of the way!" he cried. He was going to force the door. But Mama held him back. She didn't want Mr. Grasmann to hear. So then they sat on the stairs and didn't know what to do. Besides, it was cold. From time to time they tried the door again.

Down below a door opened. It was Mr. Grasmann, who was taking his dog out. The dog raised its head, sniffed, and began to growl.

"Is someone up there?" Mr. Grasmann called.

"Yes, we are," said Mama dolefully.

"Now, now," said Mr. Grasmann. "Do people celebrate Christmas on the stairs these days?"

He came upstairs, and Papa explained what had happened.

"Well," said Mr. Grasmann, "we can do something about that." He went back down to his apartment.

Papa, Mama, John, and Jonas sat on the stairs, and the big dog crouched in front of them and growled. Luckily, Mr. Grasmann came back quickly. He brought a huge ring with a number of keys on it.

"One of them is sure to fit," he said.

"That won't work," said Papa. "Our key is on the inside of the lock."

Mr. Grasmann scratched his head. "That makes the job harder," he said, "but it is by no means impossible."

Again he went downstairs, and this time they could hear that he went all the way down to the cellar. His dog remained behind.

Mr. Grasmann returned with a piece of strong

wire. "Watch carefully what I do," he said to John and Jonas. "Whoever can do this can be a first-rate burglar anytime he wants to."

"Oh, Mr. Grasmann!" said Mama, and he laughed. She had never realized that Mr. Grasmann could laugh.

He bent the wire into a loop, stuck it through the keyhole, turned and twisted, poked something, and after a short time something fell down onto the floor inside. Now one after the other he tried all the keys

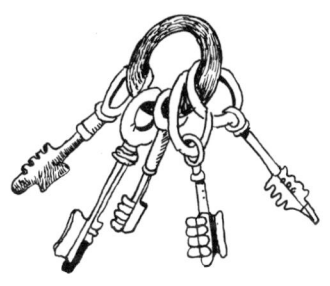

that were on the big ring. The thirty-third one fit. Mr. Grasmann opened the door.

"How can we thank you?" said Papa.

"Please give us the pleasure of celebrating Christmas with us," said Mama.

John and Jonas cried, "Yes, please!"

Mr. Grasmann answered, "For myself, gladly. But my old dog doesn't get along with people very well. Unfortunately I have to be governed by him." And he went down to the street with his dog.

John said, "The dog isn't like that at all. I was petting him the whole time."

# The Christmas List

Wolfgang and Susanne had written a number of things on their Christmas list, but one wish they underlined with thick, red-pencil lines: "One night we'd like to stay up for as long as we want to."

"Why not?" Mama and Papa had said.

They celebrated Christmas Eve together, there were lots of presents, they had something good to eat, and when it was time, Papa and Mama said, "We're tired now and we're going to bed. Good night."

"That's right," said Susanne, "and don't forget to brush your teeth."

"And don't read anymore!" cried Wolfgang after them.

"We're much too tired for that," said Mama and yawned.

When Wolfgang and Susanne were alone, they

111

jumped into chairs and stretched out their legs. Then they ate lots of marzipan. Susanne decided she should cover her parents up and give them a good-night kiss. She did so, and Mama and Papa let themselves enjoy it.

Then Wolfgang and Susanne went back to the living room and turned on the television. A choir sang endless Christmas carols, which was boring. On another channel there was news and the weather report.

"Why isn't there any children's program?" asked Susanne.

"Just think," said Wolfgang. "All the children are in bed now."

That pleased them very much.

They turned the television off again and went into the kitchen. In the refrigerator there were lots of good things, but they weren't hungry. They only drank some soda and went back to the living room. They sat down again.

"Terrific when you can stay up so late," said Wolfgang. Susanne nodded and yawned.

They read the books that they had gotten as presents and then ate some more marzipan. Susanne got more soda from the kitchen, and since she had forgotten the glasses, they drank out of the bottle. Wolfgang spilled the soda on his sweater; it was cold and sticky. He pulled it off and tried Papa's new pajamas on. Susanne thought he looked funny. Mama had received a slip, which she tried on.

"Hah, we're ghosts," she whispered. She stuck her head through the door to her parents' bedroom, but Mama and Papa were sound asleep, so Wolfgang and Susanne withdrew.

They tried television again. On every channel there was whistling and sparkling.

"It's broken," said Susanne.

"Don't be silly. They've stopped for the night. All the grown-ups are in bed now. Who would they broadcast for?"

"For us, for instance!" answered Susanne. She sat very straight in her chair.

Wolfgang turned the set off again. It was very quiet.

Once the cupboard creaked.

The light was very bright.

"How long do we want to stay up, anyhow?" asked Susanne.

"Till morning," said Wolfgang.

Their eyes burned so terribly that he turned the lamp off. He tripped over the soda bottle and fell against Susanne's chair. She pulled his hair, and it hurt. So he pinched her arm.

Susanne ran away from Wolfgang and hid in her bed. Wolfgang crept quickly under his covers so that Susanne couldn't find him.

When they woke up, it was dark outside again. Papa and Mama had been up for a long time. They had had breakfast, had gone for a walk, had had visitors, watched some television, and just done nothing.

Christmas Day was over.

# Jens's Doll

There are dolls that can sit and run, laugh, weep, and speak; they have eyes that close and hair to comb, and you can even feed them.

Jens wanted such a doll for Christmas.

Aside from the fact that Grandmama thought it strange for a boy to want to play with a doll, she also thought that those elaborate dolls were much too expensive and a simple one would do as well.

Jens got a doll from Grandmama. To be sure, it could not run, laugh, weep, or speak, it didn't have eyes that closed or hair to comb, but it was really large and looked nice. She had a little hole in her mouth that you could stick a pacifier into, and she was soft and light.

Jens was satisfied and called the doll Manuela.

He built her a house out of boxes, made her a bed out of cushions, sat her beside him at the dinner table, and let her swim in the bathtub, for Manuela was made of plastic.

On the second day after Christmas Aunt Helga and Kathy came to visit.

Kathy brought with her a new doll, who was called Olivia. That is to say, today she was called Olivia; yesterday she was called Anna Louisa; tomorrow she might have still another name. Kathy had not been able to decide definitely yet. In fact, the name Manuela pleased her too. Olivia might be called that next week.

Kathy's doll could sit and run, weep and laugh. In her back she had a little compartment into which you could stick a tiny cassette, and then she said, "Mommy, love me, I'm hungry, I'm tired."

Kathy could also feed Olivia; she had a little baby bottle from which Olivia drank. After a while Kathy changed her diapers, for Olivia had wet herself; the wetness came from the milk. Kathy washed her off with tissue, dried her, and diapered her afresh. Then she combed her hair into a new arrangement, and Olivia flapped her eyelids. In the meantime, Kathy put a cassette in her back so she crowed and laughed with pleasure.

Kathy kept playing with Olivia, and Jens suddenly found his doll boring.

"Naturally she's not as good as Olivia," said Kathy kindly, "but you can do more with Manuela than you think. For instance, if she had no pacifier in her mouth, she could drink out of Olivia's bottle."

They ran into the kitchen to the refrigerator and refilled the bottle with milk. Manuela would certainly drink more than Olivia. She swallowed and swallowed so that Jens was astounded at how much she took. Finally the milk came up out of the little hole in her mouth when Kathy tried to give the doll more. When Jens pressed on her plastic belly, Manuela spit. Kathy had to admit that even Olivia couldn't spit. Jens was proud of his doll. He took her into her box house and laid her to sleep. Manuela had become very heavy and certainly very tired too.

After some days Grandmama kept noticing that there was a strange sour smell in the apartment. She had always had a sensitive nose. When it didn't get better, she searched in Jens's room for old rolls. Sometimes he didn't finish eating at the table, took something to his room, and then forgot it. The last time it had been a cheese sandwich.

But Grandmama found nothing. The smell grew worse. Grandmama wore a thick shawl because she often threw open the window to get air.

The mailman, who liked to think he was funny, stuck his head through the door and asked, "Do you have a cow in here?"

This teasing was painful to Grandmama, for she was always clean and tidy, and she liked it when people noticed it. She left the windows open all the time, and the curtains waved in the wind. Jens had to keep his parka on when he ate, for Grandmama didn't want him to catch cold.

Three days later Grandmama had two old friends in for afternoon coffee. Naturally she closed the windows, but under the furniture and behind the curtains she put saucers of water in which she had laid lemon slices. All the same, she noticed how her friends looked around and sniffed.

"Come here, Jens," she called, to distract the friends. "Come and show us your new doll!"

"A boy who plays with dolls?" cried one of the friends loudly.

"And why not, pray?" asked Grandmama, annoyed.

The other friend took the doll from Jens and sat it on her lap. "How heavy the dolls are these days," she said. "You can hardly carry them."

"They are lighter than in our day," said Grandmama. "This one here weighs scarcely anything; she's plastic; I chose her myself."

The friend replied, "This plastic stinks terribly. It must be a new mixture that is heavy as stone."

Grandmama's voice grew louder as she said, "For forty years you've been a know-it-all." She took the doll from her friend's lap and almost let it fall. "Why is it so heavy?" she cried.

"She drank a lot," said Jens.

"And why does she stink so?" she asked.

"She doesn't stink," said Jens.

"Put her away. We'll talk about it later," said Grandmama. And she asked the friends if they would like coffee. The friends said they were a little giddy from the air there and would have to go now. That was all right with Grandmama, for she wanted to see to Manuela. Jens thought she was pretending when she held her nose. He said Manuela had

drunk milk out of Kathy's bottle, and now she always sank when she went swimming.

"Now I understand." Grandmama groaned. "She was pumped full of milk, and no air could get to it. The milk soured first, then turned to curds, and now to cheese. And in this plastic belly it all smells especially horrible."

She carried Manuela out the door. Jens ran after her and asked, "What are you going to do with her?"

"I'm going down to throw her in the garbage can," said Grandmama.

Jens began to bellow and hung onto her so that she couldn't go downstairs. Doors opened in the apartment house.

"Don't make a scene here," said Grandmama. She went back into the apartment with Manuela. Jens kept jumping up around her and trying to take the doll away from her.

"Stop that," said Grandmama, as she defended herself. "There is nothing else to do with her. She must go out. And please stop that howling. You will get a new doll. As far as I'm concerned, it can be one that can sing and hop."

But Jens only wanted Manuela. He was *so* unhappy.

Finally Grandmama understood. "Then we will operate on her. I hope she will survive!"

She opened the window wide and placed a sheet of waxed paper on the table. Manuela was laid on it. Grandmama cut her belly open, first with the paring knife, then with the kitchen shears. Now even Jens discovered that she didn't smell especially nice. Grandmama leaned out the window for a bit. In a while she held Manuela under the water faucet like a fish and flushed everything out of the stomach and down the drain. She used lots of hot, soapy water to wash her out thoroughly, again and again. Each time she would sniff her and shake her head. Manuela still smelled.

"She'll have to air a few days," Grandmama decided. She tied a string around one foot of the doll and hung her outside the window. Manuela, light as a feather and with a gaping belly, was a sad sight as she swung in the wind.

Grandmama said, "Later she'll have a bandage of adhesive tape. When she is dressed, no one will see anything."

Jens was happy and thought that Olivia, with her curly hair and the cassette in her back, would never have survived all that surgery.

He ran down to the courtyard to the other children. Rudolf had just discovered what was hanging in the window. He hopped around and screamed, "Jens has finally had enough of the doll. He's slaughtered her, and they're going to have roast doll."

Sometimes Jens couldn't take a joke. Rudolf ran away howling.

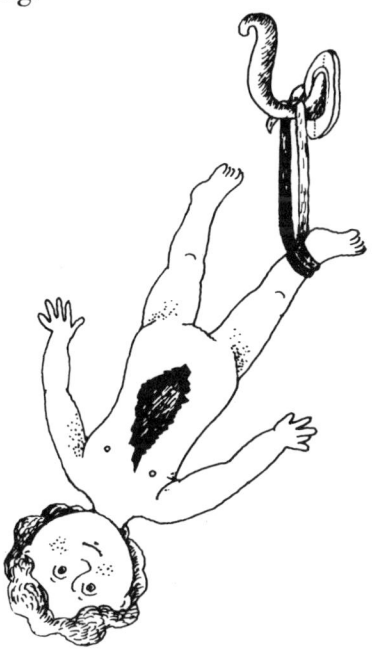

# The New House

Building a house takes a long time and is a trial of nerves. Something is always missing, something goes wrong, something isn't ready.

Mrs. Winkelmeyer said to her husband, "You've got to push the workmen to go faster. We want to be in the new house by Christmas; we can't be any later than that."

Mr. Winkelmeyer went to the building site and said to the workmen, "My wife wants to be in the new house by Christmas for sure; she can't be any later than that." He supplied a case of beer, the workmen thanked him, and, sure enough, four days before Christmas they were finished and left.

Workmen leave a mess in every corner. The house had to be scoured, scrubbed, and swept. But if everyone helps the work can be done in one day.

Three days before Christmas the moving van

came and the Winkelmeyers moved in. There was confusion on a gigantic scale. The beds were in the kitchen, the houseplants were in the cellar, the new washing machine was inside, and the upholstered furniture was outside in the rain. Mrs. Winkelmeyer never faltered. She directed where everything should be put, and soon each thing was where it belonged. Mrs. Winkelmeyer unpacked baskets, bags, and boxes. To the children she said, "Put all the papers and wrappings outside in a pile." Mr. Winkelmeyer cleared out and threw things away too. In the yard a huge mountain of Excelsior, boards, boxes, and other trash grew higher and higher. Everything that was no longer nice enough for the new house went into the pile.

In the evening Mr. Winkelmeyer tossed a match into it, and there was a huge bonfire, which the children kept poking with sticks.

Two days before Christmas all the cupboards and drawers were in order, even the curtains were hanging.

"Now I'm quite ready!" said Mrs. Winkelmeyer.

On the morning of Christmas Eve they all slept late. They stayed at breakfast until noon.

"How I enjoyed that!" said Mrs. Winkelmeyer.

The children cried out, "Do we have a Christmas tree yet?"

No one had thought of that. They all rushed to the car. It seemed to take a long time to get to the city, for the new house was some distance out in the country. Mr. Winkelmeyer couldn't find a parking space and had to leave the car a long way off in a little alley. In the meantime, the stores had closed.

The stand with the Christmas trees was empty and abandoned.

They all looked blank. The children pouted. "Without a tree it isn't a real Christmas."

Downcast, they turned around and drove home.

When they got out of the car, they saw a little tree by the front door. There was a note on it that said, "Much happiness in your new home, from the neighbors."

The children hopped up and down. Mr. Winkelmeyer carried the little tree into the house, and Mrs. Winkelmeyer said, "I'll go look for the ornaments." She ran upstairs.

Mr. Winkelmeyer set up the tree. Then they waited. Mrs. Winkelmeyer didn't come back. They called, but Mrs. Winkelmeyer didn't answer.

Mr. Winkelmeyer and the children ran upstairs. Mrs. Winkelmeyer was sitting on the rug. All the drawers were turned out, all the cupboards stood open, there was great disorder.

"One disaster comes right after another," she said. "We must have burned the box with the Christmas-tree ornaments along with the others by mistake."

She said that her nerves needed a little rest. Mr. Winkelmeyer was very quiet, which was what was always best for his nerves.

The children were whispering in the corner. Then they told their parents that they should nap for a little while. They said they would. The children ran downstairs, and Mr. and Mrs. Winkelmeyer could hear them running back and forth.

After Mr. and Mrs. Winkelmeyer got up and went downstairs, they found the prettiest Christmas tree they had ever had. It was covered with chains of paper clips and safety pins. On the branches hung Mrs. Winkelmeyer's jewelry and all the coffee spoons. And glittering at the very top was the new house key.

# The Mix-up

Some years ago Mr. and Mrs. Schmidt had rented a room to a student whom they treated like a son. They had no children of their own, although they would dearly have loved to. The little room was supposed to have been the child's room. Still they had grown old alone, and the student had lived in the little room. He had breakfasted with Mrs. Schmidt in the mornings, and in the evenings he had talked with Mr. Schmidt. Mrs. Schmidt had made his favorite dishes, and Mr. Schmidt had soled his shoes, and because he never had enough money, Mr. and Mrs. Schmidt had overlooked the rent.

Later, after he finished studying, he had married and gone away. He now had a good job some distance away.

Mr. and Mrs. Schmidt were just a little lonely.

They often spoke of the good times with their student and waited every day for a letter from him. He didn't write often. Now and then he sent postcards, if he was on a business trip. And naturally he let them know when a new baby arrived. But he didn't write long letters, and a long letter was just what Mr. and Mrs. Schmidt would have especially liked.

One thing did arrive regularly and punctually: a large Christmas package. Mr. Schmidt would collect it personally from the post office three days before Christmas. It wouldn't be opened until Christmas Eve. Mrs. Schmidt would put a candle in the kitchen window, and Mr. Schmidt would pick up the big scissors. Mrs. Schmidt always pushed him aside, for she didn't want the ribbon cut. Instead she unknotted it carefully. Mr. Schmidt sat beside her and drummed his fingers impatiently. In the package every year was something for Mr. and Mrs. Schmidt to wear. There were also good cigars, which Mr. Schmidt smoked during the holidays, and the special pralines that Mrs. Schmidt adored. They would try on the new things and be pleased that everything fit well. Mr. Schmidt would light up one of the cigars, and Mrs. Schmidt would nibble on a praline. They then spent the evening happily, full of memories. So it had always been up till now.

This year it was all different. The pullover that was supposed to be for Mr. Schmidt was too short and too tight; in vain Mr. Schmidt tried to pull it over his head. His stomach would never fit into this sweater!

"We shouldn't be ungrateful," said Mrs. Schmidt, "but he should have thought of your age a little when he picked out these colors. You could never wear those yellow and red stripes!"

Mr. Schmidt really liked them quite well, in any case better than the gray and brown colors that Mrs. Schmidt liked to see him wear.

In the meantime, she had unpacked a nightgown that was pale, thin, and filmy. Mr. Schmidt clucked his tongue, but she said, "Completely impossible! It doesn't even go to my knees, and me with rheumatism! If the doctor were to see me in it, I'd blush."

There were no good cigars in the package, only a big carton of cigarettes, and Mrs. Schmidt found no pralines either; instead there was chewing gum.

Christmas Eve wasn't as nice as usual. To be sure, Mr. Schmidt had his everyday cigar stumps, one of which he lit, and Mrs. Schmidt found a few bonbons she could suck on, but they both brooded.

"So very strange," said Mr. Schmidt. "He's beginning to forget us. That is, he hasn't forgotten us completely or he wouldn't have sent a package at all. But he's forgotten how old we are, how we look, and what we like. That makes me very sad."

Mrs. Schmidt didn't see the matter so simply. For some reason she couldn't figure out this package seemed strange to her. Usually she lay in bed and read detective stories, but now she had to think some more. Nothing was right about this package. It was packed for other people. Yes, perhaps it wasn't for them. For whom then? And if they had the wrong package—that is to say, if they had a package that was for someone else—somebody had probably gotten the one that was for them. And somewhere someone, perhaps at this very minute, was nibbling on one of her expensive pralines!

Mrs. Schmidt shook Mr. Schmidt awake. She wanted to talk with him right away. But he wanted to sleep and not discuss something he didn't know anything about in the middle of the night.

"Typical," said Mrs. Schmidt and went to the kitchen.

She put on her glasses, for she couldn't read without them, and saw on the wrapping paper that the address was correct. Obviously, or they wouldn't have gotten the package from the post office. She examined the box, but except for the colored wrapping paper she found nothing. Then she turned it and turned it, and on one side she discovered a name and a street here in the same city. Mrs. Schmidt almost put on her coat over her nightgown to hurry there that very minute. But she remembered that it was three o'clock in the morning and lay down in bed beside Mr. Schmidt. She waited, wide awake, for three hours, then got up, made coffee, and wakened Mr. Schmidt. They very nearly quarrelled, for Mr. Schmidt liked to sleep late, especially on holidays. Now he didn't even get to drink his coffee in peace. Breathlessly Mrs. Schmidt told him what she had discovered during the night.

She had wrapped the package again, tied it well, and stood before him in her hat and coat. She wanted to scream, as Mr. Schmidt slowly pulled on his boots. She wanted to shove him, as he casually walked down the stairs. She wanted to pull him, as he sauntered along the street.

At this time of day the streetcars ran only every half hour. They had to wait a long time, and then they had to ride from one end of the line through the entire city to the other. The streetcar stopped at every stop, although no one got on. They were the only passengers. Mrs. Schmidt wriggled back and forth in her seat. Mr. Schmidt sat very still with the package on his knees.

They had a good distance to walk. Twice they lost their way and had to ask children who were playing in the street. Finally they stood before the right house, and Mrs. Schmidt rang.

A young woman opened the door, a little boy bounding behind her.

"It's like this," said Mrs. Schmidt. "We have here a package we received that most likely belongs to you, and we assume that you have one that is for us. We would like to exchange them so that each gets what belongs to him."

Mr. Schmidt thought that Mrs. Schmidt spoke

somewhat aggressively and asked the boy in a friendly tone, "What's your name?"

"Robert," said the boy. "And yours?"

"Schmidt," said Mr. Schmidt.

The young woman suggested that they come in and rest and have a cup of tea. They did have a peculiar package. In it was a sweater that reached to Robert's toes, dark green, and for her a black-and-white housecoat that was three times too big for her.

"Two times," said Mrs. Schmidt.

Yes, and then there were cigars in the package, though she smoked only cigarettes. Would Mr. Schmidt like to smoke one?

"Wait, don't get excited," said Mrs. Schmidt. "First we want to sort it all out!"

"My wife is always reading detective stories," said Mr. Schmidt to the young woman.

And she answered, "So am I!"

Then she explained that her package came from her sister, who had the same name as the student who had lived with Mr. and Mrs. Schmidt, for she was his wife. The student always had been careless, certainly he had mixed the packages up during the packing. Now the young woman got the filmy night-gown and the cigarettes. Mr. Schmidt got the dark-green pullover as well as the cigars, and Mrs. Schmidt got the housecoat together with the pralines. For Robert there was the red-and-yellow-striped sweater and the chewing gum. It all worked out just right.

They drank tea together and wrote a long letter in which they reported to the former student and his wife all that had happened. Robert painted a picture story to go with the letter. He stuffed his jaws with chewing gum. Mrs. Schmidt passed the pralines around, and the two others smoked.

Robert and the young woman accompanied Mr. and Mrs. Schmidt to the streetcar. Everyone waved until they could no longer see each other.

Mr. and Mrs. Schmidt would soon have visitors.

Mr. Schmidt had always imagined a grandson like Robert.

# Elsie

Elsie tried only once to pee like her five brothers, and it went badly from the start.

On the afternoon of Christmas Eve Mother had lit the old hot-water boiler. She said that first Greg and Olly, the two biggest, should bathe, then Tim, Frank, and Stefan together, and finally Elsie alone. Tim bet that all six could fit into the bathtub. Frank said it wouldn't work. They tried it and, when they all squnched up together and hung their legs over the side, succeeded. There was a lot of splashing and almost all the water overflowed the tub onto the floor, but it was great fun. Mother banged on the door and told them to hurry; Father wanted his tea. And then afterward they would have their presents, which took a long time with six children.

They disentangled themselves, dried, and then

all ran quickly down the hall to go to the toilet once
more. Greg stood on the edge of the toilet, and they
all copied him. All except Elsie.

"You're only a girl," said Tim.

"She's afraid she'll fall in," cried Stefan.

"You don't dare," yelled Frank.

A girl who has five brothers dares to do anything. Naked and wet, Elsie clambered onto the
edge and stationed herself forward, just like the
boys.

"Look away or it won't work," she said, and

they all had to laugh. Then Elsie lost her footing and plunged feet first into the toilet bowl. At first they all laughed even harder, but Elsie was whimpering a little, so they grabbed her and tried to help her out.

Now this was no ordinary toilet. All the plumbing in that house was ancient. The toilet bowl was like a funnel, which went into a pipe on the outside of the house wall and ended down below, over a pit. There was no flush, only a pitcher of water you had to pour down.

Elsie was stuck up to the hips in this funnel. Greg, who was already big and strong, grabbed Elsie under the arms and pulled. But she stuck so fast that he couldn't raise her even a centimeter. Stefan, the smallest, ran through the house bellowing, "Elsie slid into the toilet!"

Mother came out of the warm living room into the hallway and caught him. "You are never dressed in time. Hurry, if you please, young man."

"The others aren't ready either, not Elsie either," Stefan cried defensively.

Mother ran to find them all. And there she saw Elsie.

"I can't believe this!" she cried. She tried to pull Elsie out by the hands. Elsie didn't move. She just began to scream.

"She'll have to stay in there forever," said Stefan.

Mother ordered Olly and Greg to get sweaters or something warm, since Elsie had nothing on. Then they must get dressed quickly, for soon they would have their presents.

Father sat at the set table and waited. Finally he stood up and began looking in all the rooms and hallways.

"Hey, where are you hiding?"

"Elsie is hiding in the toilet," said Stefan, who ran past him looking for his shoes. Father found Mother as she was winding a thick shawl around Elsie's neck and pulling a second and then a third sweater over her head. Elsie was whimpering, "I'm cold, I'm freezing."

"Then come out of there," said Father.

"She can't," returned Mother. She put a wool cap on Elsie.

"Pull yourselves together. We want to have tea," said Father. To Elsie he said, "Make yourself thin," then he grabbed her and pulled with a powerful upward jerk. Still Elsie stuck fast. Now nobody knew what to do. They were sorry for Elsie. Her teeth were chattering, and sometimes she whimpered very softly. Mother put a woolen blanket around her so that they could scarcely see her. "On top I'm much too warm, but underneath it's cold. My legs are like ice!"

"Good heavens," cried Mother. The pipe to the funnel in which Elsie was stuck was open underneath. Outside it was below freezing.

"Do something," she begged Father.

Father tried to phone the plumber and the auto mechanic, but no one answered at either place. They had left their workshops and gone home long ago.

Father said to Greg, "You go and get the plumber." And to Olly, "And you go get the auto mechanic."

Elsie cried louder and louder. Father said to Mother, "Give her some whiskey. This is an exception." But Mother wouldn't. Instead, she ran and got hot milk, on which Elsie burned her tongue. Now she was really howling. Father went to look for his tools. He wanted to take off the big bolt that held the funnel to the pipe.

Stefan reassured Elsie. "Father will unbolt you, and we'll take the toilet into the living room. Then we can at least have Christmas."

This didn't comfort Elsie at all, and Mother shushed Stefan. "Don't talk nonsense!"

Suddenly Elsie wriggled as much as she could and cried, "Ow, I'm so hot underneath I think I'm burning."

"Now she's delirious," cried Mother.

But Elsie wasn't. Tim and Frank had run into the yard. They wanted to help Elsie. They had laid a piece of tin over the pit under the end of the pipe. Then they kindled a gigantic fire on the tin, and the hot smoke was pouring up through the pipe.

Father had just found the wrench when he saw the glare of the fire. "Are you out of your minds?" he yelled through the window. He ran downstairs, stamped out the fire, and pulled the piece of tin off the pit. Tim, who was standing on the edge, almost fell in. Father caught him, but instead the wrench dropped in.

Upstairs Mother and Elsie were moaning, "Hurry up, please, hurry up."

Father looked in his workshop again and grabbed the biggest hammer he had. "Look out," he cried and swung.

But Mother held onto his arm because she was afraid for Elsie. So Father only hit the bowl very gently, and it didn't even crack. He tried a few times, but Mother was always in the way and he gave up.

"Where are Greg and Olly with the workmen?" he cried and ran impatiently to the telephone.

Mother ran after him and said, "You know very well there's no point in calling."

In the meantime, Stefan picked up the hammer and said to Elsie, "Shall I give it one?"

Elsie closed her eyes and whispered, "I don't care. Hit it hard."

Stefan was the smallest, to be sure, but he had strength.

The bowl split, and Elsie clambered out like a chick coming from an eggshell.

Everyone was terribly proud of Stefan.

The water in the bathroom boiler was still hot, and Elsie was put into the tub again. She whimpered a little because her feet tingled, but when they were all finally sitting around the table, she soon felt better. Mother brought the teapot and cut the cake.

About this time Olly arrived with the auto mechanic, who had attached his towing crane to his truck. He pointed to it and said, "As I understand the situation, only force will help!"

Almost at the same moment, Greg arrived with the plumber. They were carrying two toolboxes, tubing, and a cylinder of compressed air. The plumber panted, "It won't work. The pipe has to be blowtorched from underneath."

Father and Mother were very embarrassed that Stefan had already taken care of the problem, for tradesmen too like to celebrate Christmas quietly and not be called out. Of course, in an emergency they come quickly.

But otherwise they need much longer.

The plumber didn't bring the new toilet bowl until March.

# The Letter

Mama was glad when Papa and Andreas went out together on Saturday. They disturbed her when she did the housework and took care of the baby. But they were to be back in time for lunch, please. Afterward Andreas had finally to write his Christmas thank-you to his grandparents.

"Yes, yes!" Andreas called back. He didn't want to do it.

Papa and Andreas went and got gas. Then they got Mama's coat from the cleaners and sauntered around the market. At last Andreas asked to go to the antique shops. He liked to rummage around in the old stuff with Papa. Papa had to explain what lots of things were used for to him; most of them were so old that no one needed them anymore because they had something else to do the job. For instance, no one uses oil lamps anymore because there are electric lights. You never churn butter in a wooden tub anymore but buy it in packages. Who grinds coffee by hand in an old-fashioned coffee mill? Now you just stick the plug in the wall, and the coffee is ground in a trice. Andreas thought it was exciting when Papa told him how it used to be.

Sometimes they even bought something from the antique dealer. One time they had taken home a tin jug in which people used to fetch water before there was running water in every house. Another time Papa had bought a silk parasol, which ladies had carried in the olden days so as not to get burned by the sun. Of course Mama always cried, "If you've been to the antique shop, please wash your hands thoroughly," but she was pleased with everything. She had put grasses in the jug. And from the parasol she would probably make a lamp, she said.

Papa and Andreas went through a gate into a courtyard where there were a number of sheds. Along the shed walls leaned old junk: stools with three legs, tables without leaves, iron bedsteads, sleds with rusty runners, manure forks, wagon wheels, and who knows what else. In the sheds hung old clothes and picture frames; moldy boots,

broken china, clay pots, and clocks that no longer worked were stored there. Furs lay in heaps in the corners.

Papa and Andreas rummaged around through everything. Finally Papa bought a spotted little mirror in a metal frame.

"This is a spying mirror," he explained to Andreas, "which old ladies used to have outside on their window frames in the old days. Then they could sit in their living rooms and secretly watch everything that was going on in the street."

"It's like a car mirror," said Andreas.

"Yes, exactly," said Papa. "We can screw the spying mirror onto the door of the nursery. Then Mama can watch the baby without having to get up."

On the street Andreas said, "I have something too."

"A letter!" cried Papa. "Where did you get it?"

Andreas had found the letter in an old bureau. He asked the antique dealer if he might have it, and he said yes. But Andreas couldn't read the letter.

Papa said that people had written like that in

the old days. He could read the writing some, and together with Mother he would be able to decipher it.

"I can't wait to see what's in it," cried Andreas.

Of course, after lunch, Mama wanted Andreas to write to his grandparents first. But Andreas begged and nagged until Mama and Papa sat down and deciphered the old letter.

Munster, December 25, 1842

Dear, good Emilie,

Our father has said we should thank you at once for the pretty present the postman brought us from you. The cinnamon stars tasted capitally good, and we rejoiced very much over the little frocks you sewed for us. They fit perfectly.

You asked how we are. We are well. We are learning diligently with Mr. Moritz, who still has his game leg and hobbles with a stick; that is our bad luck, for oftentimes it lands on our backs. Our father, however, is of the opinion that we have probably deserved it. Dear Emilie, how much nicer it was when you taught us. We wish that you would come again and didn't have to look after your sick sister's many children. Signorina Lucca, who is continuing to teach us piano, says we are making good progress. Pauline and I can already play a sonata for four hands.

Dear, good Emilie, my Christmas list this year requested a pair of Dutch ice skates, a primer, and bonbons. I received all of these things, to my great joy.

Pauline wrote that she wanted a fur cape of squirrel first of all and with all her heart, but then besides she asked for kid gloves, a wax-headed doll, an album for pressed flowers, tiny tin doll dishes, and rose hair ribbons. She got only the fur cape, however, because that was her heart's desire. Our father is of the opinion that every child should receive presents of the same value, and her present cost as much as my skates, primer, and bonbons together.

Dear Emilie, you know Pauline and her folly! She cried because she had only one present and I had three of them. That was how she saw it. She was always foolish, my little sister, and it is difficult to make things clear to her. I will let her use my skates sometimes, read to her from the primer, and give her some bonbons.

We all think of you very warmly and miss you.

My father and mother bid us send you their greetings. Please remember from time to time,

> Your pupils,
> Pauline and Eugenia,
> who has written this letter.

Mama said, "My, that is a very old letter."

"Are Pauline and Eugenia grown up now?" asked Andreas.

Papa said, "They are long dead. Perhaps this Christmas letter is all that is left behind of them."

Andreas said, "If I write to Grandfather and Grandmother now, maybe a boy will find my letter in an antique dealer's someday." And he took special pains with it.

# Angel Marie

Little Marie was an angel for sixty years.

When she was a child she had a hard time learning in school. For this reason she had no part in the nativity play that was put on every year at Christmas by the children in the graduating class. It was an old play, with long, difficult lines. Only very good students could memorize the major parts. Still, almost everyone had a small part, whether shepherd, farmer, soldier, ox, or ass. Everyone had at least some words to say. Only Little Marie wasn't allowed to take part, for however hard she tried, she couldn't remember. It made her very unhappy.

Finally the time came to try on the costumes, which were as old as the nativity play. Each year they were mended and made smaller or larger or longer or shorter as necessary. The shepherds were garbed in coarse smocks, Mary had a beautiful mantle, and Joseph a slouch hat. The animals wore heads of papier mâché and were wrapped in real hides. But the most impressive were the wings for the angel. They were of goose feathers and reached from the floor, which they brushed with their tips, to high over the head. They were fastened on with leather straps across the chest and were very heavy.

This year the angel was played by a child who looked exactly the way you would imagine an angel to look: slim and tall and with lovely blond hair. After she had worn the wings for a whole afternoon, she burst into tears and said she couldn't stand around so long with those things on her back; the wings were much too heavy. There was nothing else to do but put the wings in a corner and make some lighter ones out of gold paper instead.

When all the children were arranged on the stage again, Little Marie, who was big and strong for her age, fastened the rejected wings onto herself. They weren't too heavy for her. She went up on the stage, stood behind the gold-paper angel, and smiled happily, with a fiery red face. And no one had the heart to send Marie away.

So this time there were two angels in the nativity

play: one who had a long speech and another who stood beside her, silent and proud.

In the spring all the other children who had been in the play left school. Only Little Marie was kept back.

So she was there once again when the nativity play was produced, and again she was the silent angel. Quite as a matter of course she took the big wings home afterward and put them in the closet behind her clothes.

Because arithmetic and reading and everything else there was to learn continued to be difficult for Marie, she was kept back a second time. Some people whispered that Little Marie had failed so as to be able to play the angel again, but that really wasn't so, for in the years following, when she had left school, Marie always appeared with her wings when the rehearsals for the nativity play began.

Now she was known everywhere as Angel Marie. The name pleased her, and she liked it when people said to her, "You really are an angel!" They said it to her often because Marie pitched in and helped wherever she could. She stacked wood, she watched little children, she took packages to the post office,

dug vegetable patches, hung up wash, stirred plum jam for hours on end, shoveled snow, polished silver, and was always at hand when she was needed.

Once she was even asked to come and give out Christmas presents instead of Santa Claus. The children were afraid of Santa Claus but not of Little Marie. She was very proud of that. At precisely the appointed time she stood at the door wearing her wings. She let the children recite poems, sang with them, and then tipped out the sack into which the parents had put their presents beforehand.

In time, more and more people wanted to have

Angel Marie give out presents. So as not to forget anyone and not to get mixed up, she carried all the information with her, written down in a little book. Marie made these appointments from the first of Advent on. Only the times for the rehearsals of the nativity play were set aside, for Little Marie placed great value on not missing a single one.

Otherwise, she hurried through the streets in every free hour before Christmas. She wore high laced boots and had the wings fastened over her winter coat. If it snowed, she protected the feathers with a rain cape, which bellied out and fluttered behind her. There were always some children hopping and jumping around her. It wasn't easy to get a date with Little Marie, for she was almost always booked up.

And, as usual, Marie took her place on the stage in the nativity play as the silent angel.

She had become quite plump with the years. Her hair was first gray, then white. Only strangers who happened to see the play wondered at the old angel among all the children.

And only people who had just come to town laughed if they saw Angel Marie on the street at

Christmas for the first time. The next year they didn't laugh, for by then they had found out that Marie was indeed an angel.

She had never married, for she thought it inappropriate. She had never heard of a married angel.

When she was no longer steady on her feet, she went into the old people's home. The wings seemed to become heavier from year to year. Still it never occurred to Little Marie to hang ones made of gold paper on her back. She still went around at Christmas with the powerful wings, gave presents to the children, and was in the nativity play.

Little Marie was an angel for sixty years.

She died last spring. They put the wings in the coffin and laid Marie on top of them, and thus she was buried.

# Sodium Bicarbonate

Sometimes Mrs. Voss came over in the morning. She said she wanted to borrow something from Mama or she wanted to ask a favor. That was surely only a pretext because they would sit at the kitchen table, smoke cigarettes, and talk with each other.

Papa said that Mrs. Voss kept Mama from her work. If she was there, lunch was never on time and nothing else was done at all. Mrs. Voss was a thorn in Papa's side.

Mama said she had a right to relax with her friends.

Then Papa banged the door shut and went downstairs to wash the car.

"Has he something against me?" asked Mrs. Voss.

"Oh, please!" said Mama.

"Yes," said Mrs. Voss, "just before Christmas

the work piles up: washing, polishing, getting ready. You don't know which to do first!"

Mama nodded. "And," she said, "if you don't keep right after it every minute, everything just gets left. Who will do it if we don't?"

Mrs. Voss nodded. "In the old days," she said, "we had more time. Now you can never get around to anything anymore."

Mama nodded.

Papa had come in looking for the big sponge. He threw in, "People who sit around never get anything done!" The door slammed behind him.

"Tsch," said Mama.

"When I think," said Mrs. Voss, "of all the things we used to bake! Remember sugared clove stars?"

And Mama nodded.

Barbara and Stefanie, who had just come home from school, said, "Did they taste good?"

"Marvelous," said Mrs. Voss. "No comparison to the junk you buy in a package today."

"Why don't you ever bake any?" asked Stefanie.

"They're too much work," said Mama.

"Too bad it's high time I was going," said Mrs.

Voss. "As I recollect, you need egg whites, powdered sugar, and some flour."

"And cloves, of course," said Mama. She had already put the ingredients on the table. "But you can't ask that much work of anyone," she said.

"It isn't so bad. Except that the dough has to be kneaded for an hour," said Mrs. Voss, beating the eggs in a bowl.

"We'd love to help," cried Barbara and Stefanie.

"You can roll out the dough and cut out the stars," said Mama. She stood there and wished she had something to do too. "Do you know crisp almond loops?" she asked.

Mrs. Voss couldn't remember them, but they sounded delicious from Mama's description. There were enough ingredients left, and Mama quickly mixed up the dough. Barbara and Stefanie cut out the clove stars. Now Mrs. Voss had nothing else to do. In any event, she wanted to wait to see how the sugared clove stars turned out. So, she said, she would whip up some cut-out cookies, which she had learned from her grandmother. She only needed twelve eggs and some flour and sugar for the recipe. But Mama didn't have a dozen eggs left.

At this moment Mr. Voss rang the doorbell. He was hungry and wanted to know when lunch was going to be ready.

"Turn right around, run to the store, and get us two dozen eggs—a few more can't hurt—who knows what we'll need them for!" said Mrs. Voss and pushed him out the door. All ten of her fingers were covered with flour, which was now brushed off on his back. "And a package of salts of hartshorn!" she called after him.

"Where are you off to in such a hurry?" asked Papa. He appeared from behind the wet car.

"To buy salts of hartshorn and eggs," cried Mr. Voss and rushed away. Papa knew what Mama made from eggs, but he didn't know why she needed salts of hartshorn. He hoped Mrs. Voss hadn't recommended it to Mama for a headache or to make his boots waterproof. Mrs. Voss was a thorn in Papa's side. He thought he had better see about his lunch.

But Mama wouldn't let him into the apartment. At the door she called to him, "Hurry up and go get some cinnamon, honey, and three kilos of sugar." And Papa got ten floury fingerprints on his back too. While the sugared clove stars were cooling and the crisp almond loops were in the oven, smelling delectable, and Mrs. Voss waited to make the cut-out cookies, Mama had remembered filled honey horns.

"Hm, they must be good," said Barbara and Stefanie. They licked all the bowls and secretly stuffed their mouths with hot clove stars.

Papa dashed down the stairs and halfway met a breathless Mr. Voss with a heavy shopping bag. But then he had to turn right around again and go to the drugstore for candied fruit peels, cardamom, and bicarbonate of soda. He caught up with Papa and asked if he knew what that was good for.

"No idea," said Papa and went with him to the drugstore.

"I hope no one is sick," said the druggist.

"Why?" asked Papa and Mr. Voss.

"Well," said the druggist, "you usually take bicarbonate of soda for a stomachache. Of course it's used for baking, too, but that's old-fashioned now."

Papa never found out if anyone was sick. Before he could ask at home, Mama had taken the pack-

ages from him and sent him to the grocery store again. This time he had to get butter, brown sugar, rum, and some more flour and eggs. It wasn't any different for Mr. Voss. They chased upstairs and downstairs, to the grocery, the druggist, and back again. And they never succeeded in getting into the kitchen.

After the stores were closed, Mama and Mrs. Voss wanted them to bang on the shutters and ring the doorbell of the druggist's home, which was next door. Altogether they had gone back and forth twenty-eight times.

"Soon you'll have bought out my whole store. What's going on at your place?" asked the grocer.

"We don't know," said Papa and Mr. Voss, exhausted.

"It could be illness!" the druggist shouted across the street. "Shall we come with you and see?"

That was all right with Papa and Mr. Voss. So they all climbed up the stairs and rang the bell.

Barbara opened the door. She was very pale, and Papa asked, "What's the matter with you?"

"I feel terrible," she said. "Stefanie too. She's already in bed."

"I knew it!" cried the druggist. "There's an infectious illness!"

Papa flung open the kitchen door. There sat Mama and Mrs. Voss at the table, talking. "Come on. We're finished," they called.

The kitchen smelled of cinnamon, rum, and cloves. Everywhere were piles of fancy cakes and Christmas cookies. The doors to the other rooms were open, and every surface was covered with plates of baked goods.

"Who wants to try some?" asked Mama.

"Well, I never!" said Papa. He was speechless. Never again would he say that Mrs. Voss kept Mama from her work.

Mr. Voss, the grocer, the druggist, and Papa ate as much as they could. Mama and Mrs. Voss didn't want any. They had licked off their sweet fingers so often that now they felt like eating only sour pickles.

"What's wrong with Barbara and Stefanie?" asked Papa.

"They have upset stomachs, but they'll be all right again by Christmas," said Mama.

"Half a teaspoon of bicarbonate of soda in water will help them," said the druggist.

# The Well-Behaved Child

Once there was a boy named Lutz who wanted to give his Mama something for Christmas. He wanted to make something or paint something or buy something with his pocket money for her. But whatever it was, he wanted her to like it.

"What do you want?" he asked, standing right in her way. She rushed about doing the housecleaning, watched to be sure nothing on the stove boiled over, telephoned once, and looked at her watch.

"Mama, ask me for something," he said. She pushed him to one side, looked for the cleaning things, opened the door for the mail, closed the window, and stirred the soup.

Wherever Mama wanted to step next, there was Lutz standing right in the way. She pushed him away from the door of the cupboard, took the chair away from him, asked him to get out of the way, and cried, *"Please*, don't bother me."

"But I only want to know what you want," said Lutz. He held tightly onto her apron.

"I only want a well-behaved child," said Mama and freed herself.

Lutz went into his room, sat on the bed, and wondered how he could get Mama something like that. To make one or paint one was pointless. But where could you buy one? And how expensive would one be?

Mama called, "Don't sit around, get up, hurry. We have to go shopping!"

Lutz walked to the supermarket with Mama.

It was huge, and they could buy almost everything there. Lutz knew his way around. He knew the aisles where the milk and cheese were, and the corner with the fruit jams. A little farther on were the breads and cakes, and at the other end the little toy cars he collected. Lutz knew where the powdered soap was and where the special orders always were. But there had never been children in the supermarket, at least not to buy.

At the vegetable counter Lutz climbed into Mama's cart. At the jams and jellies he pulled some of them down. At the meat counter he pestered Mama to push him.

"You'd better go outside and wait for me there until I'm finished and have paid," she said.

Lutz stationed himself on the street in front of the supermarket.

A little girl hung on the door handle and swung back and forth with the door. The cashier shook her finger at her, and the little girl stuck out her tongue. Lutz thought, She is not a well-behaved child. Mama wouldn't like her.

Nearby stood a baby carriage. A woman with lots of packages came by, bent over it, and said to Lutz, "Look, how sweet. That is a well-behaved child."

Lutz waited until the woman was no more to be seen. Then he pushed the carriage around the corner quickly. He ran with it as fast as he could toward home. The well-behaved child gurgled with pleasure.

The front door was shut, for Mama was still in the supermarket. Lutz put the baby carriage behind the cellar door where no one could see it. It was supposed to be a Christmas surprise. He sat on the front steps and waited. Suddenly he realized that this well-behaved child must belong to someone. Oh, well, he thought, I will buy it from them. It can't be too expensive. It's not brand-new; it's

already used. That would be cheaper. Lutz knew about that from Papa's car.

Mama came running around the corner with her shopping bag. "There you are, safe and sound! Thank heavens!" she cried and wept a little. She hugged Lutz so hard that it hurt. "That poor woman and that poor, innocent little mite! What an uproar," she said, "and you weren't there either, so right away I thought the worst. But now I have you again. . . ."

Lutz was very confused. But the well-behaved child was wakened by Mama's talking and began to scream.

"What's that?" said Mama and went over to look.

Lutz held onto her and said, "Please don't, Mama. It's your Christmas present." Mama stared at Lutz, and then he went on, "It's the well-behaved child that you asked for."

"Oh, Lutz!" said Mama.

She grabbed the baby carriage, turned it, and ran back to the supermarket with it. The well-behaved child bellowed louder and louder.

Lutz ran beside her and thought, This mustn't be the right child. It was going to be hard to hunt one up. Why did Mama have to want such a thing? Why not something else? Lutz tried to ask Mama, but she didn't hear.

In front of the supermarket stood a policeman and a bunch of excited people. Everyone was crowding around a woman who was crying. Mama pushed her way in and told the woman something, and no one paid any attention to Lutz.

In the afternoon he made a calendar for Mama because she had asked for one.

# Mr. Probst's Dream

He can never recollect having a memorable Christmas, says Mr. Probst. But, he says, in his opinion, the days after Christmas can sometimes be very memorable. That he knows.

Mr. Probst comes from the utility company. He reads the numbers on the electric meters, and then he figures out how much everyone has to pay. He is on his legs the whole day. They hurt from so much stair climbing, for he is no longer young. Perhaps for that reason he isn't especially friendly, but he doesn't mean not to be. He says the bad mood rises slowly, from the boots up, and toward evening it gets worse. Then just about everything makes him cross.

When his day is over, Mr. Probst goes home through the big shopping streets. He sees the many chains of lights that have been lit since November,

although there are still four weeks until Christmas.

"I'd like to send them a sweet little electric bill someday," he says and feels cross.

All the display windows are gaily decorated, for people are supposed to give each other everything there is to buy for Christmas, including washing machines, clothes, travel alarms, coffee cups, rubber boots, perfume, snow tires, or shower caps. "They infect themselves with buying and giving just like colds," says Mr. Probst and feels cross. Over the entrances to shops and department stores are loudspeakers dinning out Christmas songs; they come from records and tapes. Usually you can hear other songs at the same time; they overlap and mix with each other. No one pays any attention to them.

"It's no better than cats yowling," says Mr. Probst and feels cross.

On the corners stand men in Santa costumes who wait until people come along with little children. As soon as they see one, they spring out to take the child on their arm. A photographer takes pictures for a memento, which the parents are supposed to buy. Because very often several Santas scuffle over a single child, it begins to cry, and no one buys these photographs.

"Serves them right," says Mr. Probst and feels cross.

Everything he buys during this time—whether thread, soap powder, or cat food—is wrapped carefully in beautiful colored paper, fastened with transparent tape, and tied with shining ribbon. Mr. Probst must wait until the saleswoman hands him the little package with a nice smile, and his legs hurt.

"Such nonsense. Next they'll wrap each roll separately as a present," he says and is cross because at home he must carefully unwrap everything again.

He is cross because everyone is rushing and chasing, buying and carrying, out of breath and out of time.

He is cross that in the front yards electric candles burn on the evergreen trees day and night and that his daughter-in-law bought a plastic Christmas tree that you can open and close like an umbrella. She thinks it's practical because the needles don't fall.

He is cross that he receives a pile of Christmas cards and must write some.

He is cross about television and newspapers, about all the hubbub and the many preparations, and he would like to have his peace. Everyone should have some peace. It should be quiet and cozy. So Mr. Probst imagines a memorable Christmas celebration.

One day he will go to his boss and say, "I will volunteer for duty at the utility company on Christmas Eve. It doesn't bother me. Everyone else can go home."

The boss will clap him on the shoulder and say, "We know that it's a sacrifice, but we thank you, my friend."

His colleagues will wave and wish him a Merry Christmas. He will remain behind, completely alone. He will walk around and check to be sure the turbines are working right, that the control clocks are in order, and that the right voltage is going out over the wires. Naturally he doesn't know much about it, for he is only a collector, but it will go all right. He will look around him some and finally find a certain lever that he must use to turn off the current.

The whole city will be without light.

All the streetlights will be out, the streetcars will stand still, not even the traffic lights will work.

In the houses it is totally dark. The electric candles on the trees burn no longer; the lights are off.

It is also entirely quiet; no television, no radio, no record players, no tape machines are working anymore.

At first the people will be frightened. They will stumble around or trip over something as they are looking for firewood or matches. Certainly many will fumble about with fuses until they look out the window and see that everyone else is in darkness too. They will creep around and somewhere find a candle they had put away. By its light they will sit around the table. Some will be bored and not know what they should do. The children will nag, though, for they will want to go on with the Christmas celebration. There is no more music; they can't watch television either. There is nothing to do but sing themselves, which they are no longer used to doing. They must have the melodies in their ears, for they have been hearing them everywhere for weeks, but they haven't listened when the words were sung. Perhaps one or another knows a verse; otherwise, they must invent them themselves.

Perhaps the children will get their parents to play with them. There are lots of things you can play without lights.

Perhaps they'll all go out onto the stairs to find someone who knows what's wrong. They will meet their neighbors, whom they have not seen for a long time. Perhaps someone will even meet someone for the first time, although they have lived next door to each other for a year or so.

Some whose candles have burned out will knock on their neighbor's door, where a light still shows. They will sit together.

Sometime later, of course, Mr. Probst will lift the certain lever again. It will again be bright and loud.

Probably there will be a giant row, and his boss will yell at him, "You have failed, you collector!"

But that won't matter to Mr. Probst.

For the time being he is just imagining it, but sometime he will do it. One memorable time.